Thinking Big
The Story of John Biggers and Biggers Industrial Gerlinger

To
Mary Reed
from
Johnny Biggers
9-23-86

Thinking Big

The Story of John Biggers
and Biggers Industrial Gerlinger

by B. Carolyn Knight

Aristan Press
Placentia, California

Introduction

For me to enumerate even the major achievements of Johnny Biggers would require more space than is allotted me in this preface. Besides, his successes as a businessman, entrepreneur, prominent citizen and loving and attentive family man are mentioned elsewhere in this book.

Johnny Biggers can truly be referred to as a Nazarene Horatio Alger for, through incredible ability, energy, discipline and determination, he has moved from obscurity to prominence—and in so many fields.

But I write of him as a churchman and friend.

It has been my privilege to know Johnny Biggers for over forty years, meeting him first in North Sacramento Church of the Nazarene. And it has been gratifying to see him, through the years, enjoy ever-widening responsibilities and prominence in his local church and on various boards in his district, including many years as secretary on the District Advisory Board—the highest position open to a layman in any Nazarene district.

Along with his lovely wife, Esther, who has for years served effectively as District Missionary President, the duo of Johnny and Esther Biggers has made a significant contribution to their church, with their influence reaching far beyond their local church and district. And now, with the increasingly successful production of Christian video, their influence will not only be nationwide, but also worldwide.

Johnny and Esther Biggers have proved, and are proving, the scripture that states that if we seek first the kingdom of God and His righteousness all things necessary to successful and fulfilled living "will be added to us."

But I write, primarily, of Johnny Biggers as a friend—an understanding, encouraging, supportive and dependable friend. His unfailing and contagious optimism, his positive approach to people and problems and pressures, his dedication and discipline in trying always to exceed his previous best—all of these qualities, and more, have been a constant inspiration to me. And I know that I am a better man and, hopefully, a more effective minister for having known my friend Johnny Biggers.

C. William Fisher, D.D.
International Evangelist

Table of Contents

CHAPTER ONE

A Threatened Dream

I don't know about tomorrow,
    I just live from day to day.
I don't borrow from its sunshine,
    For its skies may turn to gray.
I don't worry o'er the future,
    For I know what Jesus said.
And today I'll walk beside him,
    For he knows what is ahead.
Many things about tomorrow
    I don't seem to understand.
But I know who holds tomorrow,
    And I know who holds my hand.

John Biggers lifted his voice in song, feeling a surge of exhilaration flow through him as it did each time he sang the well-loved hymn. Despite the demands of his prospering business, his long hours of community involvement and the responsibilities of his family, John had seldom missed one of these choir practices in the more than 35 years he had attended the North Church of the Nazarene in Sacramento.

His love of music and the deep contentment he received from his religion always seemed to soothe and relax him during these Wednesday night sessions. Closing his eyes as the familiar melody rose to a crescendo, John tried to ignore the sudden and insistent ringing of a telephone coming from the room next door.

Ruth Sullivan stepped out of the church office, waited for the music to end, then called, "Johnny, the phone's for you. It's Esther."

He hurried to the phone, concerned that something must be wrong for his wife to contact him at choir practice.

"Johnny." Esther's voice was shaking, and he could tell she was holding back the tears. "Someone just called and said the store's on fire."

The feeling of peace he had experienced from the music instantly left him, but he managed to remain calm.

"Now, Esther, let's not allow ourselves to get too excited. It might just be a rumor."

He assured his wife that he would drive by the shop on his way home, then replaced the receiver and retraced his steps to the choir room.

"Tessie, I can't stay. Our place may be on fire."

Tessie Freeman, the choir director and a long time friend of the Biggers, looked alarmed. "Oh, no, Johnny. It can't be true, can it?"

John rushed to the door, fighting a panicked feeling. "I don't know, Tessie, but Esther got the report, and she certainly believes it. If it's a false alarm, I'll be back."

Hurrying through the parking lot, John jumped into his 1974 Gran Torino, jammed the keys into the ignition and immediately switched on the radio.

"We interrupt our programming to bring you news of a three-alarm fire in the heart of the downtown area," came the deep voice of the KFBK disc jockey. "Firemen are now battling the tremendous blaze at Gerlinger Motor Parts on K Street."

It was true then. It wasn't a hoax. It wasn't a rumor.

He gunned the motor and pulled swiftly onto Las Palmas Avenue, his tires squealing as he turned sharply onto El Camino and headed for I-80. Taking deep breaths and using all of his self control to remain calm, Johnny slowed down and forced himself to maintain the speed limit during the three mile drive into town.

He followed the route almost automatically. After all, he'd driven to 2020 K Street almost daily since he was 17 and had begun working for Gerlinger's. He'd begun as a counterman in 1944 and was now the owner and president of the company.

An acrid smoke was filling the valley, stinging his eyes and further blackening the September sky. Dire news reports continued to flow from the radio, surrounding Johnny with their ominous predictions as he sped down the freeway to the J Street offramp.

"It appears that this blaze has completely destroyed the machine shop," said the voice of the KFBK reporter on the scene, "and firemen say that buildings on either side of Gerlinger's are now being threatened."

Johnny could hear the sirens as he turned right on K Street. He saw the police blockade a few blocks ahead and knew he could take his car only a short distance farther. Edging the Gran Torino toward the curb, he parked and began running toward 21st Street. His heart pounding in his ears and his breath short and labored, John could see nothing ahead but flashing red lights and a heavy black haze.

Stopping to catch his breath, he leaned against a parking meter and watched the flames leaping through the roof and the oily smoke curling toward the sky. Crimson sparks jumped in the furnace-like heat, and gray ashes swirled in the air before coming to rest on the sooty sidewalk and street. Small explosions that reminded John of summer firecrackers or cherry bombs joined the scream of sirens in a cacophony of sound.

He shut his eyes, trying to erase the sight. It wasn't just his shop that was being destroyed. It wasn't just his building, his inventory, his equipment.

It was his past.

It was his future.

It was his dream . . . .

CHAPTER TWO

Childhood Memories

"Johnny! Johnny, wake up."
Johnny Biggers opened his eyes and yawned, awakened by the urgent whispering of his brother.
"Okay, Glen. I'm awake," he said, already grabbing for the pants and shoes he'd carefully placed by the side of his bed the night before. He followed his brother outside, tiptoeing to avoid waking his parents or his five other brothers and sisters. Hugging himself to ward off the early morning chill, Johnny took a place next to Glen on the front porch step, and together the boys watched the deliverymen loading their trucks at the old ice house next door.

Johnny and Glen had always been inseparable—so much so that they reminded friends and neighbors of the Biblical David and Jonathon. It was not unusual, during the summer months, for the two to get up as early as 5 a.m. to spend some extra time together, watching the sun come up and reveling in the beauty of their world.

Looking back on his younger days from the perspective of adulthood, John Biggers today speaks with warmth about that by-gone era.

"With seven children, some people thought that the Biggers family was quite poor," he says. "Most homes in our neighborhood had two rooms and a bath, but we had one room and a path—and I never knew that words such as 'new' and 'shoes' even went together.

"But wealth depends on what you use for a measuring stick, and we were rich in everything that makes life happy and meaningful."

John Biggers was born on October 27, 1926, in the modest family home in Durham, California. His parents, Alvin and Bessie Greene Biggers, had moved to the small farming community from Idaho, where they lived after arriving there on wagon trains as children.

Johnny and his brothers and sisters loved to sit in a circle around their father and listen to their dad's tales of the long journey in horse-drawn wagons from Canon City, Colorado, to Boise in the early 1900s. Alvin was 13 when his parents, David and Minnie Cox Biggers, decide to leave Fremont County, Colorado with their eight children. Johnny's grandparents had caught "roving fever" after hearing reports and seeing circulars about Idaho's rich farming and goldmining. Along with eight other wagons filled with aunts, uncles, cousins and friends, the Biggers began the 1000-mile trek on May 8, 1904.

Alvin's job, as he told his children, was to drive the Biggers' team—a pair of bays named Queen and Molly and a pair of gray horses named Pet and Pete.

The determined travelers encountered many difficulties along the way, including snow so deep that they had to put their wagons on skids and slide them through the deep drifts. On other occasions, the wagon train was assaulted by driving rain storms that forced them to take shelter in abandoned homes and sheds. Still farther along their journey, the land was so dry that they would travel for days without water.

After four months, the little caravan arrived at its destination, settling in Brownlee and Sweet, Idaho, just outside Boise. It was here that Alvin and Bessie met and married. They set up housekeeping in Strawberry Glen in 1915, moved to Durham, California in 1926 and then to Chico when Johnny was six months old.

Alvin and Bessie were deeply religious and raised their children in the Church of the Nazarene. Frank, Virgil, Janie, Glen, Johnny, Zern and Ruth were all members of the Nazarene congregation, and the tenets of their faith played an important role in their childhood. The family went to church twice on Sundays and at least once during the week. Alvin taught a Sunday School class of teen-aged boys, served as an usher and was on the Board of Trustees.

The Biggers were also strong believers in the work ethic and taught their youngsters that working not only brought a dollar reward, but also a strong sense of achievement. When Johnny and Glen were 8 and 10 years old, their father made them a work cart from pieces of scrap lumber and a pair of old motorcycle wheels and tires. A bar extending four feet in front of the cart made it easy for the boys to pull it along like a rickshaw. The brothers secured an ice route and could load 200 pounds of ice on their cart to deliver to stores and businesses in the area. During the summer, they piled their cart high with watermelons or with figs from the family's giant tree and peddled their produce from door to door. Always hard workers, the boys also cleaned the church for 75 cents a week and pulled weeds at the rate of 20 cents an hour.

Glen was more thrifty than Johnny and became the twosome's banker, hiding away their hard-earned coins behind the cardboard wall of the bedroom they shared. The minute young Johnny earned a penny, he'd want to spend it, Glen recalls.

"No, Johnny," he'd reprimand his younger brother. "You've got to save part of that penny."

"But, Glen, how do you save part of a penny?" Johnny would always ask. Patiently, Glen would explain that when they'd saved two pennies, they would be allowed to spend one of them.

Their favorite purchases were made at the local drug store, where they could buy three scoops of ice milk for a nickel. Glen always insisted that they split their hard earned treat with their other brothers and sisters, and the Biggers children would sit under the sheltering branches of the big tree in their front yard and share the fast-melting dessert.

Johnny at the age of 3.

4

Johnny, right, and his brother Glen were inseparable throughout their childhood years.

When Johnny and Glen were 12 and 14, they had saved enough money to buy a cow. Not only did "Bossie" provide the family with milk, but with ice cream as well.

"The only problem with that," remembers Glen, "was that every time we'd get out the old-fashioned ice cream freezer and start cranking, the family across the street would come over and Mother would make us share. That wouldn't have been so bad, except the family had 12 little boys!"

"It was Mother's way of teaching us to be mindful of others," says Zern. "She always told us that our reward was in making someone happy."

Neatness was also a virtue at the Biggers' home, and the old adage "Cleanliness is next to Godliness" received more than lip service there.

"Until I was 5 years old, I thought that 'neck'n'ears' was one word and that clean meant red," says Johnny, who still remembers how his father scrubbed him with a rough wash cloth until his skin turned scarlet.

Honesty, responsibility and sportsmanship were also among the traits instilled into their children by Alvin and Bessie. In fact, Alvin taught his sons that good sportsmanship should even be extended to the wild game they hunted.

"Most people hunt rabbit with a shotgun," says Johnny, "but my father didn't think that was fair."

5

Armed with a rifle to give the rabbit a fighting chance, Alvin and his sons would stalk their prey and attempt to add in this way to the family's food supply. Alvin would often invite students from his Sunday School class to accompany him on these hunting trips.

"My dad thought that all boys should learn to hunt, so he'd invite those whose own fathers didn't have the time or the inclination to teach them."

Besides rabbit, the family diet depended on shad they caught with nets in the Sacramento River, on produce from Bessie's garden and on the chickens they raised. Alvin, always concerned that his family might not have enough to eat, would never sit at the table and fill his own plate until Bessie and the children had eaten.

"We might have had less during the Depression, but we never went hungry," says Johnny. "In fact, we often took food to families who had less than we did—or we'd have them over to share our meal."

John remembers his mother quoting Luke 6:38 as they shared their food in those days of hardship: "For if you give, you will get. Your gift will return to you in full and overflowing measure, pressed down, shaken together to make room for more, and running over. Whatever measure you use to give—large or small—will be used to measure what is given back to you."

These words were never more fully appreciated than on an unforgettable Thanksgiving Day during the Depression.

"Despite the fact that we didn't have any food at all, Mother set the table beautifully, and we all sat down to empty plates, bowed our heads and began to give thanks for the blessings we did have," remembers Janie. "During our prayer, the doorbell rang and we went to the door to find a large turkey and all the trimmings sitting on the porch."

Johnny can recall another occasion in 1935 when again his family had absolutely no food in the house.

"We did have three or four gallons of gas, though," he says, remembering the desperation he felt that day when he was only 8 years old. "Glen, Virgil and I decided to take the Model T Ford and drive to our Uncle Elmer's place in Durham, seven miles away. He was the foreman on a large ranch, and we knew we could go out into the field and pick some turnips and carrots. If we were really lucky, we might get an invitation to dinner."

The three brothers piled into the old pick-up, with 14-year-old Virgil, who was nicknamed "Forrest," at the wheel. No sooner had they reached the highway than they noticed a police car behind them.

"Now we were always taught to think of policemen as our friends and protectors," says Johnny, "but in this case, Forrest didn't have a driver's license, and we certainly didn't have the money to pay for a ticket."

Forrest, who like most boys his age, had quite a bit of experience driving tractors and farm equipment, drove carefully on toward his uncle's and probably would not have been stopped if it had not been for his wide-eyed younger brothers. Glen and Johnny were staring in fear at the policeman as he pulled his squad car around to pass them. Noting the apprehension on the boys' faces, the officer motioned Virgil to pull the Model T to the curb.

The Biggers brothers and sister Janie in 1937. Johnny is second from left.

"We all began to cry and to talk to the patrolman at once," remembers Johnny, who says that, after hearing the boys' sad story the policeman decided not to give them a citation if they turned around and went straight home.

Relieved that they had escaped a ticket, but worried that their trip had been in vain and that their family would probably go to bed with empty stomachs, the boys quoted scriptures to one another as they drove home, telling themselves that "God would provide."

"As if to confirm our faith, Mom had somehow gotten a sack of flour by the time we got there," says Johnny. "And we arrived home to the wonderful aroma of biscuits and gravy."

The Biggers' brothers and sisters still rave about their mother's homemade gravy and about her ability to make delicious soup out of nothing but potato peelings. But, when it came to making biscuits, their father received the applause.

"When Mom made them, they were okay," says Johnny, "but when Dad made them, they were 'gen-u-wine' company food."

The close-knit family enjoyed the togetherness they shared and spent many happy hours playing checkers and dominoes around the big dining room table.

"Mother was good at creating games, too," remembers Ruthie. "She often made up writing and spelling games that were fun, but educational too."

"I don't think I've ever known a happier or closer family than we were," says Glen, who, nonetheless, has to admit that there were times when he and his brothers and sisters would require discipline.

"Daddy would thump us on the head with his thumb if we did something naughty like make noise during the church service," says Zern, "but Mother could say more with a look than with words, and we'd straighten up fast."

For more severe offenses, such as arguing among themselves or using slang, Bessie Biggers would march her offspring outside to choose the willow stick that would then be firmly applied to their bottoms.

"But Mother would never raise her voice to us," says Ruthie, "and tears would run down Daddy's cheeks whenever he'd have to spank us. I think it really did hurt them more than it did us."

Holidays were very special occasions for the Biggers. A patriotic family, they purchased six American flags each Fourth of July, stuck them in the radiator holes on the hood of their car and proudly drove to the Grange picnic and then to the Chico Airport to watch the fireworks display.

Each Christmas their father chopped down a huge pine tree to display in the family livingroom, and gifts would consist of rag dolls that Bessie made as well as kites, wooden trucks and wagons made painstakingly by Alvin.

"Our parents couldn't waste money on toys," says Janie, "so there would be no 'store-bought' gifts under the tree unless friends in the church gave them to us."

Easter was the holiday that Johnny Biggers and his brothers and sisters remember the most. Bessie insisted that all her children wear white for purity on that holy day and spent weeks making duck pants as well as shirts and dresses from flour sacks for her large family. Using the soap she'd made from lye and pig lard, Bessie scraped chips off the big bars, dissolved them in water and washed and bleached the clothing for days—and on Easter Sunday she would look with pride at her seven children, all dressed immaculately in starched white brilliance.

The warm circle the Biggers provided for their children offered them enough love and care to protect them from most of the ravages of the Great Depression. However, the devoted parents could not shield their family from illness, and during the early 1930s, seven members of the clan were struck with scarlet fever. The Biggers were quarantined for 35 days, and only Alvin and Johnny managed to escape the disease. The only person allowed to leave the house each day was Alvin, who knew his family's financial survival depended on the $30 a month he earned working for the WPA.

Each day while his father was at work, Johnny would climb into bed with Glen, hoping that he would contract the disease while his brother had it.

"We were so close, we wanted to be sick at the same time so that we could be well at the same time," explains Johnny.

Their attempt at togetherness didn't work during that instance, however. And three years later, when Johnny did come down with scarlet fever, he got more than he'd bargained for—he was stricken with pneumonia at the same time and was quarantined for 36 days.

Fearing for their son's life, Johnny's parents took him to doctor after doctor, and were given the same prognosis by them all.

Johnny's heart had been severely damaged.

Even with prescribed bed rest, they were told, Johnny would probably not live past his teenage years.

Despite a dire diagnosis, Johnny overcame a debilitating illness.

CHAPTER THREE

Overcoming the Odds

Thirteen-year-old Johnny Biggers sat in his bed, pillows propping up his overweight and bloated body. More than a year and a half of complete bed rest had turned his strong and wiry young frame into a puffy caricature of its former self. Except for trips to the doctors and the visits of tutors from Chico State College, Johnny's life had taken on a lonely and boring sameness.

No more games of "Kick the Can" and "Hide and Seek" with his brothers and sisters. No more running laps around the "race track" he and Glen had fashioned in the side yard. No more climbing the enormous fig tree and walking across its huge limbs from the roof of the house to the roof of the garage.

He missed the camaraderie of his junior high school buddies. He missed the companionship he and Glen had always shared. And, most of all, he missed the opportunity to live rather than merely exist.

However, the doctor had been firm.

"You must not leave your bed," he'd admonished. "Exercise of any kind will put a dangerous strain on your already weakened heart."

Johnny faithfully heeded the doctor's advice, staying in bed month after month and adhering to the strict and meager diet that had been prescribed. Doggedly he would chew the lettuce he was allowed and jokingly call it his "steak" or his "bowl of ice cream."

One day in early 1939, Bessie walked into her son's room and announced some visitors.

"Johnny, Mr. and Mrs. Thorp are here to see you."

The Thorps had been friends of the Biggers for many years, and Johnny welcomed them with a happy smile.

Howard Thorp patted John on the shoulder. "Johnny, we've just been talking to your Mom and Dad about a new doctor that might be able to help you."

Johnny's eyes met his mother's as their friend excitedly spoke of a revolutionary new technique used by a local chiropractor.

"Dr. Whitbeck uses some new-fangled electronic equipment to send electric vibrations throughout the body," said Mr. Thorp. "I can't pretend to understand it completely, but I've heard some wonderful testimony from folks who have had the treatments."

Knowing that the Biggers could ill afford the daily visits

"It's hard by the yard, but it's a cinch by the inch."

required by the doctor's innovative procedure, Howard Thorp and his wife had discussed their friends' financial problems with Dr. Whitbeck, who agreed to treat Johnny for half his customary fee. The Thorps, in a loving and generous gesture, offered to pay the remainder of the bill.

The chiropractor's advice was radically different from the admonitions the other physicians had given the boy.

"I want you to start walking short distances," Dr. Whitbeck told Johnny. "And mild exercise will help you regain your strength."

Soon Johnny's body began to respond to the new therapy, and he was able to go back to Central Junior High School to attend his graduation ceremony. Because he'd gotten sick during the second month of seventh grade, Johnny had missed almost the entire two years of intermediate school. Yet he'd kept up with the other students through studies provided by his tutors, and that June proudly walked to school to rejoin his classmates and receive his diploma.

Johnny was upset, therefore, that his friends didn't recognize him. When the other boys and girls found out the sickly looking youngster among them was Johnny Biggers, they were astounded.

"Hey, how can you graduate?" they jibed. "You haven't been to school for two years."

Johnny hung his head and fought the feelings of inadequacy and inferiority that threatened to overwhelm him. Then he straightened his back and took his place among the other eighth-graders. He'd been through too much to give up now. He'd finally been given permission to become a participant in the world again, and nobody was going to stop him.

"I made a decision that day," remembers Johnny, "a decision I promised myself I'd always keep. I decided I'd rather burn out at 15 than rust out at 95. No more sitting on the sidelines of life for me."

Surreptitiously, he began expanding the liberal limits of Dr. Whitbeck. When his family was gone, he jumped on his bike and rode the two-wheeler for blocks. With his pulse racing from the exertion, he'd hurry home, put the bicycle back in the garage and hop into bed before the rest of the family arrived home. He knew he felt much better after exercising, so how could it be bad for him? What's more, the fat he'd accumulated began to melt away and his muscles again became firm.

Johnny's progress was brought to the attention of yet another physician, a doctor practicing in Sacramento who asked the young man to participate in another innovative new study.

"You'd be one of the first patients in northern California to be tested on a new machine called an electrocardiograph," said Dr. Hepplewhite, who also suggested a diet and exercise plan for Johnny—as well as freedom from the high doses of digitalis the teenager had been taking for years.

Within eight months, John's health was much improved, and he entered Chico High School determined to excel.

John's heart condition was not the only adversity the Biggers family had to face during the 1930s. Alvin, who had to struggle to feed his large family during those lean years, managed to find a job as an automobile mechanic at a Studebaker dealership in town. One day, while manually cranking a car that he was repairing, the

"Great people are ordinary people with extraordinary amounts of determination."

vehicle backfired, knocking the crank out of his hand and striking him in the body. The accident injured Alvin's hip and, because the company refused to take responsibility for the mishap, he was unable to pay for medical help. In constant pain, Alvin could no longer continue his employment and was forced to move his family to a one-room house at the edge of town.

"It would be nice if I could say I'd been brought up in a log cabin like Abraham Lincoln," jokes Johnny today. "Unfortunately, though, my parents couldn't afford anything that elaborate."

Bessie attempted to make the tiny house a real home for her family, and softened the blow of having outdoor plumbing by carpeting the path to the outhouse with remnants of some old red carpet she'd managed to acquire.

"I'll never forget how the neighbors laughed at that," says Johnny. "But it's just another example of how I was always taught to be optimistic and to make the best of any situation."

With faith and perseverance, the family managed to survive those bleak months. Alvin's injury was finally properly diagnosed as a dislocated hip by Dr. Thomas R. Haig, who promptly put his patient in a hospital in Sacramento and, using the expertise he had developed during World War I, performed the surgery that would once again allow Alvin to walk without pain and to take on odd jobs as a mechanic to see his family through the Depression.

In the summer of 1940, Alvin Biggers had an opportunity to move to Sacramento, where a family friend had suggested he take out a construction loan to build a house. "By paying yourself for carpentry fees, you'll be able to provide Bessie and the kids with a real home for the first time and be paid a salary in the process," he was told.

It was almost too good to be true, but it was an opportunity Alvin couldn't afford to turn down. So on a hot July day in the first year of a new decade, Alvin, Glen and Johnny prepared to leave Chico to begin the construction of a new 900-square-foot home. As they kissed Bessie and the others good-bye, they promised to build the house as quickly as they could so they could send for the rest of the family before school started in September.

Waving good-bye, the three headed for Sacramento to begin a new chapter in the life of the Biggers family.

CHAPTER FOUR

Oh, Johnny

> Oh, Johnny. Oh, Johnny.
> How you can love.
> Oh, Johnny. Oh, Johnny.
> Heaven's above.
> You make my sad heart jump with joy.
> And when you're near, I just can't
> Sit still a minute. It's just
> Oh, Johnny. Oh, Johnny.
> Please tell me dear
> What makes me love you so
> You're not handsome, it's true
> But when I look at you, you're so . . .
> Oh, Johnny. Oh, Johnny, oh!

Johnny Biggers walked down the hall of the high school, and several giggling girls—including his sister, Janie, and their neighbor, Virginia Haynes—sang the new song that Wee Bonnie Baker and the Orrin Tucker Orchestra had made so popular.

Despite his embarrassment, he had to admit that the hit tune had helped him get acquainted and make friends. He'd been determined to make a new start. He'd been determined to be more like his popular big brother, Frank, whom Johnny looked up to because of his involvement in student government and his prowess on the school's boxing team. And, most of all, he'd been determined to leave his "sick boy" image behind him forever.

And he had.

He'd grown strong over the summer, helping his father and Glen build their new house at 520 Lampasas Street. They had constructed the garage first, so that they could have some place to sleep while they completed building the house. He was proud of the way he'd helped with the shingling, the framing and the hardwood floors—and even more proud of the finished product. The first house the Biggers had ever owned was more than adequate for the large family—and it was sturdy. When Alvin Biggers learned that the building code required two nails in each joist, he insisted that his boys hammer in four.

"Our house won't squeak," he told his family.

Things were certainly looking up for the Biggers. Johnny and

Glen, once more inseparable now that Johnny was back on his feet, were again saving the money they earned from paper routes and yard work. But this time they had their sights a little higher than on buying ice cream or a cow. This time they were saving for a car—a car of their very own. Each week they would excitedly count the money they had saved together for so many long months. Their father had insisted that they not only have money for the original purchase, but also enough for the car's upkeep. After all, tires and engine repairs were expensive—and gasoline cost a steep 19 cents per gallon.

After a year and a half of painstakingly saving every nickel, dime and dollar they earned, Johnny and Glen finally had stashed away enough, and it was two very proud teenaged boys who drove a 1924 Star Car into the driveway of the family home in 1939. The little coupe was equipped with a rumble seat and a wolf whistle and was guaranteed to drive on three wheels in the eventuality of a flat.

Johnny and Glen were in high spirits each morning as they drove themselves to Grant High School in their hard-earned automobile. In the manner of military pilots who painted slogans on their war planes overseas, the boys took white shoe polish and scribbled silly sayings on the fenders of their prized possession. Never knowing what to expect from one week to the next, their family and friends would laugh at the inscriptions, which ranged from "Is that your nose, or are you eating a banana?" to "Kiss her. Don't be bashful" and "We'd speed, too, if we had a car like that."

Johnny was now a sophomore and, while he enjoyed school and maintained As and Bs in all his classes, he was a highly ambitious young man and sought the challenges of a real job.

His mother had always hoped he'd feel led into the ministry. In fact, she'd named him John for that very reason and had always called him her "little preacher boy." During the time he'd been bed-ridden, his mother had fostered her dream, reading the Bible with her son and hoping God would send a sign to guide Johnny toward a future in the church. Despite the fact that John was very religious and very church-oriented, however, he never felt the calling that was necessary for a Nazarene to enter the ministry.

But what career path should he follow?

Johnny's fascination with automobiles began at a young age.

This past summer he'd had a taste of carpentry. And, while he had felt a great sense of accomplishment in the home he'd helped build, he was certain he didn't want to pursue a construction career.

He really didn't want to be an automobile mechanic like his father, either. He liked being around cars and enjoyed a little tinkering in his spare time, but the prospect of standing over, or lying under hot, greasy engines all day was not one Johnny relished.

Then what could he do for a living? All he knew for certain was that he wanted to enter a business that was people-oriented. Johnny remembered when he was 6-years-old and walked to school every day past Howard Thorp's Tire Recapping Service. His little friend, Jay, was the Thorp's son, and he'd often go inside the store to visit. He enjoyed the smell of rubber and the neat rows of tires and supplies. He enjoyed the congeniality of the customers and the "man talk" he encountered there. It was his first exposure to the world of business, and it was one he found as exciting now as he had then. He'd like to be part of a similar enterprise, he decided. And, because the automobile was now a common denominator among people of all walks of life, a job in the automotive industry would afford him the opportunity to meet many interesting men and women.

The first step to any employment, however, entailed getting permission from the high school to continue his schooling while holding down a full-time job. Despite the fact that he wanted to work, he did not want to give up his education. His mother and father, who had only gone to school through the third grade, had instilled a strong desire in all their children for earning a high school diploma.

Receiving authorization to attend classes while working 33 hours one week and 40 the next was an involved process. Johnny spoke to each of his teachers and to his principal, who in turn took his case before the school board.

When the approval finally came, Johnny approached Bob Lowe, the owner of Globe Auto Supply and, at the age of 14, began his life-long affair with the automotive industry.

"I'll always remember my first day on the job," says Johnny. "My first customer wanted a set of brake linings for a Model A Ford and, since I'd received absolutely no training, I had no idea where to begin looking."

Parts of every size and description were stocked in large bins throughout the store, and the inventory was listed in an oversized, mysterious book behind the counter. Distressed by his inexperience, Johnny hurried to the cafe next door, where his boss was enjoying a cup of coffee, and asked for help.

"I've never forgotten to this day that the part my first customer wanted was a WB310 for $2.95," says Johnny, who vowed that day to memorize more part numbers than anyone else.

Johnny continued to work at Globe even after he graduated from high school at the age of 16. He traveled around Sacramento for his employer, picking up parts from various automotive houses, becoming acquainted with their owners and impressing them with the neat appearance he made in his immaculate white coveralls.

One of the shops he frequented was Gerlinger Motor Parts. He came to respect George Gerlinger as an honest, innovative and

Johnny began working at Globe Auto Supply when he was 14.

straightforward businessman with high principles. George had an excellent reputation, and the machine shop he ran was clean and well-equipped.

"After much thought, I decided I wanted to stay in the parts industry," says John, "and I also decided that I wanted to spend my working life at Gerlinger's."

Unfortunately, the proprietor, who referred to himself as a "hard-headed Dutchman," had other ideas.

"He told me that, in the first place, he'd never hire any more 'kids,'" remembers Johnny. "And, in the second place, he'd never hire me away from Globe, which was one of his customers."

George Gerlinger couldn't help but be impressed with Johnny, however. Once, when he stopped by Globe and asked for a part for a Chevy he was repairing, the teenager jumped at the opportunity to wait on him. Though Johnny didn't have the particular part George needed, he offered him a comparable part for a Pontiac, telling the older man that it was interchangeable. Not believing that the boy knew what he was talking about, George bought the part, nonetheless, and was quite surprised to find that Johnny had been right. This scenario was repeated for a second time some weeks later, and George was once again impressed with Johnny's knowledge and expertise.

Each time Johnny came into contact with Mr. Gerlinger, he reiterated his desire to work at his automotive shop, and each time he

Church activities have played an important role in John Biggers' life since an early age.

was turned down. Undiscouraged, Johnny told George that he was determined to work for Gerlinger's someday because it was the best parts store in town.

"I'll be back," he told George, leaving the "hard-headed Dutchman" shaking his head in bewilderment.

Despite the fact that he was working 50 to 60 hours a week, Johnny always found time for church activities. Besides worship on Sunday mornings at the Sacramento North Church of the Nazarene, Johnny accepted an invitation to join the choir at another Nazarene Church, which performed on a radio show each week.

Always a music lover, Johnny liked the opportunity to sing in the choir during his leisure time and also enjoyed the chance to meet other young people who shared his interest and his faith. It wasn't long, however, before John was drawn to the Wednesday night group by more than "a song and a prayer."

"What first attracted me to Esther Debler was the fact that she was so wholesome," says Johnny. "In fact, if I had to describe her, I'd say she was 'spic'n'span.'"

Nicknaming her "Squeaky Clean," Johnny enjoyed teasing the vivacious brown-haired girl and inviting her ready and good-natured laugh.

Esther didn't return Johnny's attempts at flirtation, however—at least not at first. She was engaged to a serviceman, and the ring she wore on her finger symbolized the promise she'd made to marry the soldier when he returned home from overseas.

Not that such a technicality deterred Johnny.

On the Fourth of July in 1944, Esther's and Johnny's churches gathered for an old-fashioned Independence Day picnic at a nearby ranch. The two teenagers teased and joked with one another all day, and that afternoon were placed on the same team for a softball game. Never much of an athlete, Johnny took a lot of ribbing from Esther, who was an excellent player and whose pitching abilities earned her the moniker "Rubber Arm." In contrast to Esther's athletic ability, Johnny missed fly balls, stumbled over line drives and struck out at home plate.

Johnny took Esther's teasing with good humor, and the next time they shared the outfield, he began returning her jibes.

"I'm going to catch the next ball that comes this way," he told her.

"What do you plan to use? A bushel basket?"

Johnny just smiled. "If I do catch the next ball, will you kiss me?" he asked.

"Sure," Esther replied flippantly, feeling assured it was a no-risk situation on her part.

With such an exciting incentive, however, Johnny not only caught the ball and collected the kiss—but he also won the girl.

Esther and Johnny began dating quite seriously after that fateful softball game, attending church activities together, going hiking, and joy-riding in Johnny's newly purchased 1938 Oldsmobile.

"I'll never forget that car," says Johnny. "I had it painted such a dark blue that it was almost black. It was my pride and joy, and I think Esther fell in love with it before she fell in love with me."

With gas rationing a reality during the war, however, there never seemed to be enough fuel to do much driving. Johnny and Esther

Johnny and his 1938 Oldsmobile.

Esther Debler Biggers, second from left, with her brothers and sister.

would often meet with their friends Albert Dodrill and Elinor Casto, Bob Larson and Lois De Board, Vivian Larson and Tommy Syftasted, Bob Meadows, and Ted and Eleanor Hawkins to play table games. Sometimes the fun-loving group would pool their gas ration cards, jump into Johnny's car and go out to dinner.

Gotthilf Debler, Esther's father, was appalled that his daughter was wearing one young man's ring while dating another. He insisted that she make a choice and soon noticed that Esther's finger no longer flashed a diamond. With his strong feelings of integrity and his sense of fair play once more intact, Gotthilf gave his blessings to the happy young couple, and Johnny was soon as at home with the Deblers as he was with his own family.

Esther was also a member of a large, close-knit clan. She was one of eight brothers and sisters and, since both parents worked, she was responsible from an early age for much of the housekeeping chores and for having a hot meal started on the stove by the time her mother and father got home in the evening.

Gotthilf and Christina Debler were a hard-working couple and expected much from their children—Andy, Pauline, Ida, Elsie, Esther, Rolland, Lawrence and Violet. But they were also loving and devoted parents, and laughter was a familiar sound emanating from their home. The family would often gather around a large jigsaw puzzle on the living room table, and, as they fitted piece after piece together, the children loved to hear their parents tell the story of how they had come to America.

Gotthilf had left his native Romania in 1916 by stowing away on a ship headed for the United States. When his defection was discovered, he was given the choice of being deported back to Europe or of joining the United States Army. The choice was a simple one for the earnest young man. He immediately "Americanized" his name to George and willingly joined the armed forces, soon earning the status of corporal, despite the fact that he spoke only broken English.

Esther's mother, Christina Kurtz, was also from Romania,

Johnny fell in love with Esther Debler, above, because of her "wholesomeness." The young couple married in 1945 and moved into a tiny, two-bedroom home on Eleanor Avenue.

though she and Gotthilf had not met there—even though they had lived in villages 60 miles apart. Christina emigrated to the United States in the early 1900s with her first husband and settled in North Dakota. where her first four children were born. When the youngest was only 3 years old, Christina's husband died of Bright's disease.

The young widow soon met Gotthilf, who was now a neighbor in North Dakota. The two married in 1922 and for the next 14 years traveled from Colorado to Wyoming to Montana, supervising sugar beet ranches. During those years, Esther, her sister and two brothers were born. In 1936, the Deblers moved to California and established roots in Sacramento, where both Gotthilf and Christina went to work for Libby's Cannery.

The Deblers always held a deep and abiding love for their adopted country. Gotthilf became naturalized because of his service in the Army, and Christina studied for years to become a citizen, a deed she finally accomplished when she was in her 40s. Esther was brought up speaking both German and English. However, when World War II broke out, Esther's father called his wife and children together and told them that, from that day forward, there would be no more German spoken among the Deblers. They were American citizens and they would show their loyalty in every way they could—even by avoiding the German language in the privacy of their own home.

By early 1945, Johnny and Esther had decided to get married, and Johnny again began to consider his future in the auto supply industry. Once again he approached George Gerlinger—and once again he was rebuffed.

Mr. Gerlinger had a strong penchant for what he called "correctness," and even if something were "almost right," it was wrong.

"It would not be right to hire you away from a customer," he told Johnny again and again.

To prove his convictions about working for Gerlinger, Johnny took the most decided action he could think of—he quit his $35 a week job at Globe Auto Supply. Almost immediately, the young man—who was well-known by now for his dedication and strong sense of responsibility—was offered a job at the Red D Service Station, at the phenomenal salary of $60 a week, plus commission.

It was tempting, but before accepting the generous offer, Johnny decided to speak to George Gerlinger one more time.

On a Saturday morning in May, John drove his Oldsmobile downtown and walked into Gerlinger Motor Parts. A machinist by trade, George was working a lathe when he saw the persistent John Biggers enter the shop. He couldn't believe that John wanted to work for him so badly that he'd quit Globe.

"I want to work for a firm that exemplifies my own strong ideals," Johnny told George, going on to expound upon Gerlinger's excellent reputation, his customer service and his unequaled business principles.

Further surprising George Gerlinger, John offered to begin working at the shop without pay.

"I'm so certain that I'm going to be your best man that I will begin working for nothing," said Johnny. "You're an honest man and I know you'll pay me what I'm worth, so I don't think there

"To succeed, never accept the first rejection. Don't take no as the final answer. Selling doesn't even start until someone says no."

22

will be a problem."

Though the shop closed at noon on Saturdays, George and John continued talking until late into the afternoon.

When George finally got up to lock his doors and head for home, he turned to look at the tall, thin boy who radiated a self-assurance that belied his young age.

"How would you like to begin on Monday?" he asked.

George and Ella Gerlinger, at left, opened their motor parts store in 1940 at 1424 J Street.

CHAPTER FIVE

A Sacramento Legacy

Gerlinger Motor Parts, the company that had so captured the imagination of young Johnny Biggers, was founded in 1940, a year that the nation's 131 million citizens hoped would signal an end to more than a decade of hardship and a new beginning of prosperity for their ailing country.

The rest of the world was at war, and the radio waves were crackling with reports of the Germans invading Denmark...Norway...Holland. The Germans declaring war on Britain...on France. The Germans bombing London...blockading England.

Despite the still floundering economy and the uncertainty in the world, America's free enterprise system was still a viable force, and it was in these troubled times that George and Ella Gerlinger took advantage of the opportunities and promises offered in a new decade by opening the doors of their new motor parts store on April 1, 1940.

The proprietor, George Gerlinger, came from Dallas, Oregon, and a family that included a long line of industrialists. Their enterprises ranged from Gerlinger Steel and Supply to the Bank of Oregon and to the Gerlinger Carrier Company, which later merged with Tow Motor and Caterpillar. The family also owned a railroad roundhouse and repair shop, which was later sold to Southern Pacific.

George had been orphaned at an early age. His father died in a railroad explosion when the boy was only two, and his mother died shortly thereafter. Raised by an uncle, George quit high school after his sophomore year and, at the age of 15, became an apprentice for Southern Pacific. At the suggestion of his uncle, George moved to Redding, California, to further his experience and education in the family's steel company and then, as a journeyman machinist, he moved to Sacramento to work once again for Southern Pacific.

The work was not steady, however, and George found himself alternately laid-off and rehired as the fortunes of the railroad company waned and prospered.

In 1928, he went to work as a shop foreman for Colyear Motor Sales, a warehouse distributor that was the forerunner of Napa Stores. It was here he met Ella McBrayer, an inventory control clerk for the automobile supply shop. The young couple fell in love

A Model A truck was used for pick-ups and deliveries as the small motor parts store prospered.

and soon married.

It didn't take long for George to prove himself "a genius on machinery" and, within a short time, he had quite a following among the Sacramento locals. Encouraged to open his own shop, George rented the lower floor of a small building at 1424 J Street and proudly hung a sign that proclaimed "Gerlinger Motor Parts." George and Ella surveyed their 14 ft. by 14 ft. shop with smiles on their faces. It was sandwiched between a Chinese laundry on one side, a weights and measures scale shop on the other and was topped by apartments on the second story. Yes, it *was* small. And it *was* crowded. But it was a start.

As if to prophesy the successful enterprise their shop would become, George and Ella served their first customer almost three weeks before their store officially opened. On March 13, as George stocked shelves and Ella painted shelving bins, a man entered the front door and asked for some supplies he said he couldn't get elsewhere. George looked through his inventory, found the needed items and sold Oliver Kallen a water pump kit, a king bolt set, tie rod ends and a gasket set for $8.01.

Eighteen days later, with Ella taking on the duties of credit manager, a counterman serving customers and George doing the actual machine work, the new business opened its doors.

The Gerlingers purchased a little Model A truck to use for pick ups and deliveries, and Ella would often use it to run errands for their growing business. One day as she pulled up to a stop sign, a sleek Buick slowed beside her and Ella noticed a former neighbor looking down her nose at her.

"Do you drive that thing?" the snooty woman asked.

"I'll drive anything with wheels that will get me where I'm going," replied Ella, gunning her motor and leaving the Buick in the dust.

Both Ella and George knew where they were going, and servicing their private customers plus the many gas stations and garages in the area kept George and Ella quite busy. Within a year they had eight employees, and by 1942 the business had grown to such a degree that the couple rented the space occupied by the laundry next door. Tearing down the dividing walls, they were able to dou-

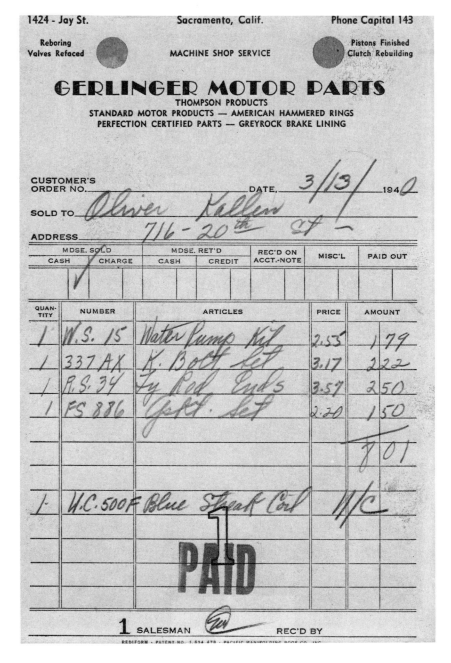

The first bill of sale for Gerlinger Motor Parts was written before the store even opened.

*Ella Gerlinger,
third from left,
took on the duties of
credit manager
for the small firm. Below
is a view through the
front window from the
machine shop.*

ble the size of their prospering firm.

"It was not easy to keep help during those days," remembers Ella. "All of the young men were being drafted. But to keep up with our thriving business, we needed two countermen and five machinists, plus George."

One of their employees, Frank Mencarini, began with the company in 1941. He was 19, had just graduated from Sacramento High School and came with a strong recommendation from his former shop teacher, Ralph Kendall, who became a Naval Commander and who, during the war, was the protector of San Francisco Bay against U-boat attacks.

"I was hired as a pick up and delivery man," says Frank, "but, in those days, a deliveryman not only picked up and delivered jobs, but helped work on them, too."

Frank was expected to strip brake shoes, clean components and do whatever else was necessary to get the parts ready for the machinists.

During the war years, it was difficult to find employees to work in the machine shop, since so many young men were serving in the war.

"George was a good man, and he expected a lot from his workers," says Frank. "I worked many more than 40 hours a week, including weekends—and all for a $20 a week wage."

Frank's tenure with the company was interrupted by a call from Uncle Sam in 1942, and he left Gerlinger's to serve a three-year stint in the Air Force.

As in cities across the United States, Sacramento became enmeshed in the war effort. Families planted victory gardens and saved their pennies to buy War Bonds. Youngsters collected scrap metal for the cause, citizens volunteered for positions as air raid wardens and men in uniform were a common sight on the streets.

Two air bases, Mather Air Field and McClellan Field, were activated when the war broke out in Europe, and another military installation, Sacramento Signal Depot, was opened in 1941 for storing and repairing army and electronic equipment.

The war was making it harder and harder for Gerlinger's to furnish supplies and parts to its customers, and bearings were virtually impossible to find. George decided to open a Re-Babbiting Service down the alley from his machine shop to repair worn engine bearings. One of George's employees, Lloyd Fisher, managed the shop, which was deluged with business from the first day. Melting the old babbit off, recoating the part with nickel, lead, silver and tin to give it strength and then cutting it down to size was a profitable enterprise during the war years. However, the rebuilding process was more expensive than manufacturing the parts new, so when the war ended and bearings were again available, the shop was closed.

Post-war Sacramento brought an immense population boom to the state capital. With the influx of people came new factories, new housing tracts and cars, cars, cars. Old country lanes were widened and improved to accommodate a new generation on wheels. And while George Gerlinger's shop had been the sixth parts house in Sacramento when it opened in 1940, after the war there were 125 similar shops within a 20-mile radius.

Despite the increased competition, Gerlinger's had built a solid and respected reputation, and by 1948 even with the increased space created from leasing the laundry next door and the scales company on the other side, there wasn't enough room to fulfill the shop's burgeoning needs. George began looking around for a larger location and found a perfect lot near the corner of 20th and K Streets. The land, a mile east of the state capitol, was dotted with three two-story houses, but the owner was willing to remove the residences and custom build a machine shop and sales office to fit George's special requirements.

Borrowing lug boxes from CPC Cannery and additional trucks from personal friends, George's employees packed and moved equipment and supplies the seven block distance to the shining new home of Gerlinger Motor Parts, Inc.

Directing his three countermen where to place some supplies in the new facilities, John Biggers moved a few cases of automotive chemicals and surveyed his new surroundings. Just as he'd predicted, he'd become George Gerlinger's right-hand man. He laughed now as he remembered how George had looked at his fresh-faced new employee seven years before and had gruffly

"Practice does not make perfect. Imperfect practice creates imperfect results. It's only perfect practice that brings perfection."

instructed him to grow a mustache so that he would look older. The facial hair had grown in so light that Johnny had been forced to darken it with the stick of charcoal he'd found among his sister's artist supplies.

No need for such pretenses now. Johnny had proven himself, regardless of his youth. In fact, he'd recently been promoted to store manager. Johnny smiled again. Just as he'd known all along, Gerlinger's was moving ahead in the world. And he was glad to be aboard.

Gerlinger Motor Parts moved into new facilities at 2020 K Street in 1948.

CHAPTER SIX

Years of Growth

John Biggers stood behind the counter of the still new 13,000 sq. ft. building that housed Gerlinger Motor Parts and smiled as a customer opened the double glass doors and headed toward him.

"Hi, Sam. How's your little project coming?"

"Morning, Johnny." Sam shook his head. "I don't know. Rebuilding this old Packard is beginning to be more trouble than it's worth."

John laughed. "What do you need to replace this time, my friend?"

The long-time customer leaned against the attractive counter and took a list out of his shirt pocket.

"Well, let's see here. I need a set of valve springs, a couple of valve keepers and some bearings."

Johnny leaped into action.

"A set of valve springs for a '49 Packard-6. That's 12-VS419 at 87 cents each. A pair of valve keepers. That's LK 93 at 30 cents each. And bearings. That's CB 243 at $1.62 each."

Sam shook his head again, this time in amazement as Johnny went from bin to bin collecting the needed parts.

"I don't know how you do it, Johnny. Those parts are for a car almost 10 years old. You're quicker than a parts book."

Johnny smiled. He'd kept the promise he'd made to himself almost 15 years before and had learned not only the parts numbers, but also the prices of just about every item in stock. Whether someone came in for gaskets or rods, valves or brake linings, Johnny could help them immediately with his vast knowledge of parts for almost any automobile on the road.

Despite the fact that he was now vice-president and general manager at Gerlinger's, Johnny still loved to get behind the counter, roll up his sleeves and wait on the customers. And he had to admit it, he loved to show off his skills at reeling off parts numbers.

Having a photographic memory was a gift he enjoyed.

It had certainly come in handy the Sunday before when he had received a call from a man in Fresno who wanted John to meet him at the shop so that he could buy special parts for his Continental Harvester. Despite the fact that the store was normally closed on

Sundays, Johnny arranged to meet the man at Gerlinger's after church. He realized that it must be a very important purchase, because the man had chartered a private plane to get to Sacramento for his "shopping spree."

Renting a cab to take him downtown from the airport, the man met John at the appointed time and made his purchases quickly. Before an hour had passed, Johnny had filled the order and bagged the parts for a B 427 Continental Harvester engine. He shook the man's hand and waved as the taxi pulled away from the curb then walked back into the showroom and switched off the lights. As he turned to lock the doors, he noticed that his customer had left one of the bags behind.

Johnny's first impulse was to jump into his car and chase him, but he didn't know in what direction the man had gone—or to which of the city's airports. Closing his eyes tightly, Johnny relived the scene that had just occurred and, by doing so, was able to reconstruct the numbers on the side of the cab. Luckily, and in typical "parts man thinking," he had noted the phone number of the cab company as the vehicle had pulled away. Three digits had indicated the front main bearing of a Plymouth and two of the numbers had corresponded to those of an engine rod bearing from a Dodge. Though he had laughed to himself that those parts would never work together, his mental game now helped him remember the phone number he needed. He called the Checkered Cab Company, explained the problem and, within minutes, the taxi was headed back to Gerlinger's to retrieve the forgotten merchandise.

Johnny smiled now at the recollection. The man from Fresno had been so pleased he'd even given Johnny a $5 tip.

Johnny really enjoyed serving the company's industrial customers. Though Gerlinger's had gained an excellent reputation as a machine shop and was considered a well-rounded automotive jobbing enterprise, much of the firm's business could now be classified as industrial, involving engines and machinery from the aircraft, agricultural and food industries. Gerlinger's now serviced ranch equipment, as well as trucks and tractors for the Division of Forestry and for lumber mills in the Sierras. It was also the principal supplier for a fleet of 52 Caterpillars for a large corporation in northern California. In addition, parts from conveyors, oil fields and construction equipment were common sights in the company shop.

Besides the inside staff, George employed a group of outside salesmen who acted not only as order-takers but as Gerlinger ambassadors. The company's first sales force had a trading area that encompassed only a 20-mile radius. Now, however, Lou Horvath, Larry Byrnes, Floyd Sallee and sales manager, Paul Wilson, had large territories of 100 to 200 accounts each from the Oregon border on the north to the Nevada border on the east and as far as Modesto and Manteca to the south.

Business was going so well that George had branched out in the late '40s, opening a second motor parts store in the old Masonic Hall on Del Paso Boulevard. Ray Gough, who had formerly been a member of the outside sales staff, managed the shop and store, which was opened to serve customers in the north part of the city and to pick up business that the downtown location might not

> *"The customer may not always be right, but the right customer is never wrong."*

Johnny had become the
Gerlingers' right-hand man,
just as he'd predicted, left. The
store's office staff included,
below left, Bill Chappell,
Anneliese Heimburg, Lloyd
Fisher and Linda Taxara.

Below is Frank Mencarini,
who began with the company
in 1941.

35

attract. The company was growing in other ways, as well. Soon after they'd moved to K Street, George Gerlinger had started a forklift leasing business—one of the first of its kind in Sacramento. Now, when the steel-fingered machines broke down at one of the canneries or other local industries, George was able to rent the company one of his fleet of forklifts while he repaired theirs.

Diversification took other unique forms, also. Because of George's interest in boat racing, the firm became the northern California distributor of Higgins Power Boats, a popular line of inboard and outboard crafts. John F. Kennedy's PT boat was a Higgins, Gerlinger salesman would tell their customers. To accommodate the vessels, a 40-ft. by 80-ft. warehouse building was added to Gerlinger's new complex, and now a display of pleasure boats greeted customers entering the motor parts store. Many "racing types" were attracted to the Gerlinger shop during this time, among them Billy Vukovich, Mario Andretti, Gordon Johncock and Johnny Rutherford, plus dozens of other world class gold cup racers.

Racing boats of the "Crackerbox" variety had been a passion with George for years and, in 1950, his 265-cubic inch displacement inboard speedster won the National Championship race at Oakland's Lake Merritt. The boat, named "Miss Beverly" after the Gerlingers' daughter, surpassed a speed of 75 mph and won the American Power Boat Association's award for highest points in the United States that year, allowing George to secure the coveted U.S. Shield on "Miss Beverly's" bow.

Diversification took many forms as Gerlingers grew— such as in the distribution of Higgins Power Boats.

John Biggers accompanied George to many of the races and, because he was developing quite an interest in photography, loved to capture the thrill of the competition on film. His expertise enabled him to become a mediator during disputes, and his camera provided undisputed evidence if questions of rule infractions arose or when boating accidents took place.

One time John accidentally super-imposed one of George's races over footage he had taken of a downed plane. Embarrassed by his mistake, John tried to sidestep George and Ella each time they tried to pin him down to a time they could see the home movies. Finally, Johnny could procrastinate no longer, and he felt humiliated as the screen showed speed boats careening over, under and into the wings and fuselage of the crashing airplane. His red face was short-lived, however, and he was soon laughing along with the rest of his audience.

"That's the most hilarious film we've ever seen," the Gerlingers told him later that evening.

Because of the increase in Gerlinger's industrial clientele, George decided in the early 1950s to install a hard chrome plating department. The top executive traveled from Salt Lake City to Los Angeles, inspecting the few such installations in operation. As he rode back to Sacramento on the train after his "fact-finding missions," George would sketch the departments he'd seen, paying strict attention to the detail and improving on his sketch pad the equipment he had studied.

In 1950, Gerlinger Motor Parts, Inc. proudly unveiled its new

As business grew, so did the staff at Gerlingers.

electro-chrome plating process. Though it was the sixth of its kind in the western states, it was unique because it used several of George's own mechanical innovations. For instance, in some processes the crankshafts being plated had to rotate at high amperage with low voltage. This created a problem in transferring electrical current from the buss bars through the rotating device and into the equipment. George incorporated a special fixture that used liquid mercury, which allowed the necessary transfer of electric current.

Another problem George had noticed while inspecting other hard-chrome facilities was that a by-product of the process was chromic acid fumes. Heated to an intense 100- to 150-degrees Fahrenheit, the chrome produced fumes that not only had an objectionable odor, but which also impaired the breathing of anyone working nearby. Other companies, George had observed, used fans to blow these noxious and dangerous fumes away from employees, but this method wasn't good enough for Gerlinger. Though ecological considerations were not often made by employers in the 1950s, George called in an air conditioning company and commissioned it to build a hood-like device over the chrome plant equipment to "vacuum" the fumes into a catching basin on the roof, where they were sprayed with a fine mist and neutralized with barium.

The new chrome-plating department reconditioned machine shafts and other industrial equipment that had been constantly eroded by metal-to-metal wear, making it even better than new with an unusually high efficiency rating that could make the part last four to five times longer than the original part. Hard chrome jobs began flowing into the Gerlinger plant from widely scattered sections of the United States. Hawaii, which had no hard chrome facilities anywhere on the islands, was a constant source of business, and harvesting equipment from sugarcane plantations became a familiar sight in Gerlinger's new plant.

Because chrome was non-toxic and did not oxidize, food processors began sending their equipment to the plant for refurbishing. Chrome plating large crankshafts from tractors and earth-moving machinery also increased business. In addition, the State of California found that using the hard chrome plating procedure on its compaction molds assured them of accurate readings when they tested the earth fill, under the state's highway system.

As the Gerlinger reputation spread, contracts were captured for more unusual work also.

One day a cardiologist made an appointment to see George to discuss a diagram he'd brought with him. The specialist was interested in finding someone he could trust to make an intricate piece of equipment to aerate blood during heart operations. Taking several ounces of titanium, George painstakingly worked to the doctor's specifications and fashioned the first blood-oxygenator and filter ever invented. It so pleased the cardiologist that he asked Gerlinger to prepare several more.

"George and John were very hesitant to do so," remembers Ella Gerlinger. "Knowing that the lives of very ill patients depended on the new and mostly untried machine, George declined, explaining that Gerlinger's was not qualified to do medical research and suggesting that the doctor find a chemist with mechanical ability to perfect the aerator."

> "Avoid making a decision until all of the facts are in. Then make a firm decision."

Nonetheless, others in the medical community continued to seek the services of the Gerlinger staff—including veterinarians. One Placerville vet, whose clientele included small farm animals and goats, approached Johnny about fashioning an operating table that would utilize hydraulic equipment to help manipulate the heavy animals when anesthetized. The invention worked so well that veterinarians at the University of California at Davis ordered a similar operating table with a hoist that would lift up to 6000 pounds. The operating table that Gerlinger's built to those specifications aided University doctors to accomplish with much greater ease surgeries on elephants, zebras, horses and rhinoceroses, among other heavyweights.

Many other challenges were offered to the Gerlinger craftsmen, also. In the late '50s, Dr. Anton Nirchel, the dean of the engineering department at Sacramento State University, approached Gerlinger's and asked George to create an engine test laboratory for the college's engineering department. Excited about the prospect, the company offered a bid on the project and, though it was the lowest proposal, it was still higher than Sac State's budget would allow. That news didn't deter John Biggers, who with the help of several local factories, offered grants to the university, bringing the bid down and making the construction of an internal combustion engine test laboratory facility possible.

"Dr. Nirchel wanted new diesel and gasoline engines of the same configuration and horsepower so that students could compare lugging power, torque, acceleration and deceleration," remembers Johnny. Comparisons would be made with the use of 12 thermocouple connectors to test 12 different variables.

George Gerlinger and Lloyd Fisher built the entire lab facility, with state of the art manometers, flow meters and all required ancillary.

"We furnished everything except the building," Johnny says with pride of the largest job Gerlinger's had ever had to that date. "The equipment we provided was the forerunner of computerization, giving the same information, though not as quickly."

John loved the excitement and variety afforded him at Gerlinger's and daily reaffirmed the decision he'd made so many years before to carve out a career at the motor parts firm.

Taking care of customers' needs and keeping the goodwill of the people he served were always John's goals.

"If you treat a person right, when he's ready to do business, the chances are it will be with you," says John, citing the case of a Mr. Mitchell, who first came to Gerlinger's in the early 1950s.

Mitchell, owner of Mitchell Avionics in Chico, wanted information about used dynamometers, power absorption units that measure an engine's output of horsepower.

John said he didn't know if used ones were even available, but Mitchell seemed adamant that he was not in the market for new equipment and was seeking information only.

"Gerlinger's policy has always been that the customer may not always be right, but the right customer is never wrong," says Johnny, "and I had a feeling that Mr. Mitchell might someday be that right customer."

Promising to search for information on the requested equip-

"Failures were never devastating to me. They were opportunities to learn."

As Gerlingers' reputation spread, artisans were asked to work on a variety of projects.

The company received contracts from throughout California, as well as Hawaii, and the sales staff increased to include, bottom from left, Lou Horvath, Larry Byrne, Floyd Sallee and Paul Wilson.

41

ment, Johnny said goodbye to Mr. Mitchell and immediately began making phone calls to manufacturers and businesses that might have used dynamometers. Most units he located, however, were either badly worn, too old or too highly priced.

"When I called Mr. Mitchell to report this and to give him the prices of new dynamometers so that he could make comparisons, he told me he didn't want me to spend any time or money locating dynamometers for him.

"I just wanted information. I don't plan to buy from you."

Nonetheless, Johnny's intuition told him Mitchell was the kind of customer to take care of—and that sixth sense proved correct. When the executive had gathered all the information and had shopped around, he decided to purchase new dynamometers from Johnny.

"And he ended up buying six, not three," says John. "It was the largest order of its kind Gerlinger's had ever filled."

The excitement Johnny encountered in his profession didn't always come from big sales or inventive projects, however.

"The job even afforded me the opportunity to play cops and robbers," says John, remembering the time he and George left the shop one night to see a blue flash zip by and careen around the corner of the building next door.

"What in the world..." In unison the two men cried out and looked at each other in amazement as they realized that it was the company truck they'd seen flying by.

Charging out the back door without locking it, they jumped in Johnny's recently purchased 1948 Ford.

"Hurry, Johnny," urged George as they roared through the alley toward 20th Street. Braking for only an instant as he and George looked both ways to locate their stolen vehicle, Johnny turned left when he saw the truck at the next intersection.

Normally a quiet, well-mannered and law-abiding citizen, Johnny shifted into second and raced off, blinking his headlights, honking his horn and screaming out the window for the thief to stop.

The fearless twosome of Biggers and Gerlinger followed the truck and its illegal driver all the way to the opposite side of town and back to 15th and O Street, until they finally "got their man."

"The driver of the car in front of the pick-up slammed on his

"Aim high.
It's no harder on the gun."

GERLINGER MOTOR PARTS

GILBERT 2-1837

2020 KAY STREET, SACRAMENTO

brakes, trying to figure out what all the noise and confusion was about," says Johnny. "So our stolen truck was sandwiched between that car and mine."

George immediately jumped out of the car and onto the running board of the truck. He reached through the window, pulled the keys from the ignition and grabbed the young driver from behind the wheel. Simultaneously, Johnny rushed to the trunk of his car, reached for the tire iron, in case he should need it to subdue the thief and ran to the nearest house to call the police.

"I was so excited that I forgot I had the tire iron, so when a woman answered the door and saw my distraught state and the 'weapon' in my hands, she screamed and started to slam the door in my face."

Johnny hurriedly threw the tire iron down, explained the situation and asked the frightened woman to call the police department.

The incident ended happily, with the thief going to jail and Johnny and George, with their truck recovered, feeling like heroes.

"It was just another day in the exciting life of the motor parts business," says Johnny with a wink, "and I'm only half kidding. Coming to Gerlinger's was one of the best decisions I ever made."

John Biggers and Professor Richard Stockwell look over the equipment Lonnie Lunsford and Johnny designed for testing hydraulic components.

CHAPTER SEVEN

A Family Affair

"My goodness. Look at all of those darling babies. Are they all yours?"

Johnny and Esther smiled at one another as they jostled their four little ones into the restaurant for an after church brunch.

"Oh, yes. They're certainly all ours," said Esther, holding tiny Calvin in the crook of her arm and following Johnny, who was herding the twins and little Curtis to the large padded corner booth at the back of the coffee shop.

Once settled, Johnny looked around at his large happy family and felt his emotions soar. Life was going as well on the homefront as it was at the shop. He and Esther had exchanged rings on April 20, 1945, and had spent the first five years of their marriage getting established in business and building a home. Gotthilf Debler had loaned the young couple money for a down payment on their first house, a tiny two-bedroom place on Eleanor Avenue. Esther had left her job as a mail clerk for Sacramento Northern Railway when she married Johnny and had taken a new position at the Motor Vehicle Department, a situation she held until becoming pregnant.

The babies began arriving in 1950, and within two years and nine days, the Biggers family had expanded to six. Curtis was born on April 17, 1950, twins Marlene and Merlene on March 5, 1951 and Calvin on April 26, 1952.

Johnny and Esther just glanced at each other and laughed each time someone exclaimed about so many babies in so short a time.

"Well, I always have been production-oriented," Johnny loved to joke.

Actually the four little ones were exactly what the happy couple had ordered. From the time they were first married, they had dreamed of the time they could afford to start their family.

"We always said we wanted a son, then twin girls and, finally, a second son," says Johnny, pleased that his and Esther's wishes had been granted.

As the Biggers children grew, they were brought up with a strong sense of family responsibility, yet with pride in their own individuality. No one was allowed to call the little girls "the twins." Each was called by her name and was treated as a very special and

Johnny was a proud young father to twins Marlene and Merlene, above, and to toddler Curt and baby Calvin, right.

unique person in her own right. Each of the boys was encouraged to excel in his own way and at his own pace also. Their closeness in age made them highly competitive, and Esther and Johnny attempted to channel the rivalry in productive ways, such as on the basketball court or on the wrestling mat.

To prevent the jealousy that seemed almost inevitable in children born so closely, Esther called the twins and little Calvin "Curt's babies." Curt proudly held and fed his little sisters and brother and was pleased to show them off to visitors who came to "ohh and ahh" over the latest arrivals.

As the little ones grew, Curt took on the job of guardian angel and was extremely protective of his siblings— especially Marlene and Merlene. In turn, the twins looked up to their big brother from an early age, and an experience when they were all toddlers will explain why. When the girls were 2-years-old, they awakened one morning to a very hot and stuffy room. Thinking that things would be cooler if they covered the floor heater, the twins climbed out of their cribs, opened their chest of drawers and spread three dozen freshly laundered diapers over the electric heater. When smoke— and then flames—began spreading through the room, the frightened little girls climbed back into their cribs and hid their heads. Three-year-old Curt, who heard the commotion, ran into his sisters' room, began beating the fire with his blanket and soon had the situation under control. Only then did the young hero awaken his parents to let them know what happened. After praising her son and repairing the damage the fire had caused, Esther turned the entire situation to her advantage.

"Well, girls, you've burned all of your diapers. I guess it's about time you begin using the potty chair."

And, thus, Marlene and Merlene were trained overnight.

From the time they were very young, the children were educated in ways that would continue throughout their lives.

"Even when they were little more than babies, for instance, they learned about tithing to the church," says Johnny, who, nonetheless, did not want the children to feel deprived because of this tenet of their faith. Therefore, when allowances were earned, the children received 11 cents instead of 10 cents, 28 cents instead of 25 and 55 cents instead of 50.

"That way they could give the church 10 percent and still have a shiny dime, quarter or half-dollar left to spend as they wanted," says Johnny.

When the Biggers children were old enough to earn their own money, they were encouraged to do so by their parents. The boys had paper routes and yard work and the girls earned money by babysitting, helping their mother around the house and by planning and preparing a special meal each week.

Family togetherness was important to the close-knit family, and Sundays were always considered "Family Days." Vacations were rare in those early years, however. John's job was very demanding on his time, and Esther began working in the food service department of the school district when the children were all in school.

"When we did get a chance to get away for a week, it was tremendous," says Calvin today, looking back with fondness on a trip to Tahoe the Biggers took in 1962. "We kids had all earned several dollars that we wanted to take along. I had a new wallet and told Dad that I wanted to carry my money myself."

Calvin, by his own description, was an adventuresome and very

A strong family life has always been important to Esther and John Biggers.

active child, and it was with some trepidation that his father agreed to his request.

"If you want to be responsible for your own money, that's fine," Johnny told him, "but if you lose it, it's gone."

And gone it was. Cal lost his wallet on a carnival ride on the first day of the vacation.

Johnny agonized all night about his son's loss. "I lay awake for hours trying to decide what to do," he remembers. "Calvin needed to learn a lesson about responsibility, but the little guy was devastated. Was I being too strong of an enforcer? I finally settled the issue in my own mind by sticking to my guns with Cal, but filtering money through the other kids so that they could treat him to other activities."

Calvin has since had an opportunity to reflect on the lessons he learned from the loss of his money.

"When my own daughter, Julie, was 9, my wife, Barbara and I took her to Pier 39 in San Francisco. She had a new purse and wanted to carry it herself," says Cal. "It was the same story just 20 years later."

Yes, Julie lost her purse on the carousel. However, it contained not only her money and a small Bible, but also a $2000 dental appliance that the little girl wore to bed every night.

"I was frantic," admits Calvin, whose first concern was that he'd only made three payments on the dental appliance and now would have to buy another. "Then I sat down on a bench and asked myself how my dad would handle this situation."

Besides the similar instance when he was 10 years old, Calvin recalled a more recent experience he'd had with his father.

"Dad had just bought a new Bronco with four-wheel drive, and he and Curt and I decided to take off to the mountains to play in the snow. However, the first snow bank we hit caved in the whole side of the truck."

John and his sons got out to survey the damage. The Bronco had less than 200 miles on it, and the three were shattered. Cal and Curt were silent, waiting for their father's reaction.

"Well, I don't know about you two, but I'm not going to let this ruin my day," said Johnny. "We came here to have fun, so let's go."

They'd had a wonderful day, Cal remembered now as he sat on the bench wondering what to do about his daughter's lost purse and its valuable contents.

He opened his mouth and heard his father's words telling Julie that they weren't going to allow the loss of her purse to ruin their good time.

"However, we are going to have a little talk about responsibility later," he warned her.

Calvin was pleased with the way he handled the problem with his daughter and credits the lessons he learned from his parents.

"If parents invest the fundamentals into their children, the children can make withdrawals later—and that's just what I did."

The Biggers children learned many other lessons from their mother and father. When it was time for them to own their own cars, Johnny and Esther insisted that they buy older cars with manual transmissions—and that they help pay for them.

"The boys each had two paper routes, and they helped one

another deliver the Bee, the Union and the Chronicle to pay their share," remembers Johnny. "We worked together to repair the engines. I passed on lessons I had learned from my father when he was an automobile mechanic, and Esther prepared and sewed new upholstery, so it was really a family project."

Merlene enjoyed working on the engines of the family cars even more than her brothers did and could often be found with her head under the hood alongside her father. Her love of things mechanical persists even today, and she now works beside her husband, Ron Mencarini, fine-tuning the engines of the stock cars the two enjoy racing.

Besides doing things together, Johnny believed it was also important to give each of his children individual attention. When they were small, they took turns going to work with him on week-ends. They all remember how excited they felt on those special days.

"Dad would buy us soft drinks from the Coke machine and would let us take imaginary rides on the forklift," says Curt.

Marlene and Merlene enjoyed going to the shop with their father just as much as their brothers. And, despite the fact that their parents emphasized their individuality, the girls thoroughly enjoyed being twins. They were the subjects of a book about twins authored by a neighbor, Dr. Mildred Dawson, and reveled in switching places on dates or in the classroom and in playing all the practical jokes that twins historically concoct.

One night, however, the joke was on them.

"It was during the summer when we were 14 years old," remembers Marlene, "and Merlene and I decided to sleep outside on the patio because it was so hot."

The children often "camped out" on steamy Sacramento nights, feeling safe in the River Park area where they had lived since 1952.

"We didn't even lock our doors in those days," says Johnny. "Doing so would have been an insult on the integrity of our neighbors, and besides we had several police officials living nearby."

Imagine the Biggers' shock, then, when the girls let out a blood-curdling scream in the middle of the night and came crashing into the house. Hearing their daughters' chilling outcries and almost inarticulate babblings about "a man outside," Johnny grabbed the nearest thing he could use as a weapon, turned on the front and back porch lights and looked around. Suddenly he was greeted by Bill MacKenzie, the Biggers' next door neighbor and a police lieutenant.

"Did you catch him, Johnny?"

"You mean you saw him, too?"

"Yeah, but I can't find him now."

The two men searched the yards and bushes to no avail, then sat down with the girls to reconstruct the scene—a scene that still brings tears to the eyes of the Biggers family; tears of laughter, however, not fright.

On that fateful summer night, Marlene and Merlene were awakened by the pitter-patter of rain on the aluminum patio cover under which they slept. Being "good little girls," they were concerned about the clothes that were hanging on the revolving clothes line in the yard and one of the girls ran to grab the sheets and towels

Esther Biggers is involved in community service, also. Here she conducts a Missionary Convention during her eight-year tenure as Sacramento District Missionary President.

49

before they got soaked.

At the same time, Bill MacKenzie was awakened by the rain, also, and looking out his window, saw a "prowler" in his neighbors' backyard. Grabbing his service revolver and not taking time to dress, he rushed to the Biggers' yard and onto their patio.

"It was almost like the plot of some old-fashioned Keystone Kops comedy," says Esther. "Our neighbor had seen one of the girls taking clothes from the line, and the girls had seen him sneaking around in his underwear to catch the burglar. We still get a big laugh out of that story every time we remember it."

The younger Biggers all agree that they share many happy childhood memories. "The family that prays together stays together" could well be a phrase coined to symbolize the Biggers' experience. All of the children grew up in the North Church of the Nazarene and were active in youth activities and missionary programs. From an early age, religion was an important part of their lives. When Curt had an accident during his fourth birthday party and cut his finger so badly that the doctor wanted to hospitalize the youngster overnight, he refused to stay. It was his turn to recite

The Biggers clan has grown with the marriage of their children and the arrival of grandchildren. Posing for a family portrait below are, front row from left, Calvin, holding Julie, and Barbara; and Merlene and Ron Mencarini, holding Angela and Chad. Back row, from left are Jean holding Brenna, Johnny and Esther, Curt, holding Breann, and Marlene.

some memory work in church the next morning and he didn't want to miss that opportunity, his mother remembers.

Curt's devotion to his church continued through his teens, when he was honored for his stewardship by being elected to the Nazarene's International Institute in Estes Park, Colorado.

"Church was always a happy place," says Curt, "and that's why we always enjoyed it and why we all still go."

Indeed, the entire family is still active in their religious commitments. Johnny has been the director of congregational music since 1946 and has served on the church's Board of Stewards, Finance Committee and Steering Committee. In addition, he has been active in coordinating the Nazarene's Laymen's Retreats on the district level and served three terms as district chairman. He also was elected to the Sacramento District Advisory Board, which he served as secretary for 16 years. Esther has taught Sunday School classes, has served as her local church's missionary president and was a member of the district-wide missionary council for 17 years, eight of which she served as president. Curt is on the church board, is chairman of the athletic committee and serves on the executive building committee and as head usher. Marlene, who has inherited her father's musical ability, is very active in the choir and occasionally doubles as the church pianist and soloist. She often sings duets with her father and has been heard on radio station KEBR. Cal was elected to his local church board and then became the Christian Life board chairman. He's also served as a member of the district Christian Life board, composed of representatives from the 66 churches in the Sacramento district. Merlene is also an active member in her church, along with husband Ron Mencarini and their children.

"We were raised with love by parents who were both firm and fair," says Cal, speaking for them all. "They demanded a lot and had high expectations for each of us, but we cherished our childhood and will always value the love we received, the morals that were instilled in us and the lessons we learned from the most wonderful parents in the world."

"During the quarter-century of its operation, your firm has contributed significantly to the economic stability of a vital and growing section of our state. This has been achieved by attention to the needs of business, industry, agriculture and individuals, a sense of responsibility and a desire to deliver satisfaction."

Thomas H. Kuchel
United States Senator

CHAPTER EIGHT

Milestones

Twenty-five years. Two and a half decades. A quarter of a century!

April 1, 1965, was approaching and Gerlinger Motor Parts would be observing its silver anniversary. Excited by the company's upcoming milestone, the Gerlingers and Johnny Biggers were determined to celebrate in style.

Besides the week-long series of events and the gala open house that featured live demonstrations, door prizes, refreshments and films, Johnny decided to surprise the firm's founders with a civic dinner.

He booked a large banquet room at the Sacramento Inn, solicited telegrams and letters from everyone from the state's governor to local friends and businessmen and began contemplating ways to keep the festive affair a secret—not an easy task with 200 dignitaries, family members and colleagues involved.

"On the morning of March 27, Johnny called and asked if we had plans for dinner," remembers Ella Gerlinger. "We didn't see each other socially too often, so the invitation surprised us. It surprised us even more when he included our daughter Beverly and her husband, Jim."

Ella admits that she and George had "an inkling" that a small surprise party in their honor was awaiting them as they climbed into their car that evening and headed for the prestigious hotel.

"Your success, I know, has been occasioned by hard work and imagination over the years and you are most deserving of all the benefits. More importantly to me has been your fine friendship over most of these 25 years and I know that it is the reflection of your personal qualities which has given your organization its reputation for service and courtesy and community progress."

F.P. Flint, manager
Bank of America

George and Ella Gerlinger proudly celebrated the 25th anniversary of their business in 1965.

"Having been a life-long resident of Sacramento and seeing the city prosper and progress, I know that it is due in no small part to the soundness of the community made possible by businesses such as yours. I know that you must be proud of the achievement that has been accomplished by you and the people working with you during the past years. I know that as time progresses you will continue to be a credit to the business community and the life of Sacramento."

Edwin L Z'Berg
California Assembly

Their suspicions became even stronger when they passed their friends, Ray and Lou Chatfield, on the freeway, heading in the same direction. Nonetheless, Ella and George were completely unprepared for the ballroom full of smiling guests who stood to applaud them as they entered and took their places on the dais.

Looking out into the audience, they were overwhelmed and proud to see state legislators, county officials, the mayor, city representatives and hundreds of friends, customers and business associates there to present them with verbal bouquets for their 25 years of achievement.

"George was a shy, retiring man and, though he was pleased, he was also embarrassed by all the attention," says Ella. "When it was his turn to address the audience, all he could say was a modest thank you."

"In this period of continued growth and expansion in our No. 1 state of California, we look to firms like yours as an essential part of a balanced pattern of development for the future."

Edmund G. Brown
Governor

Judge Peter Manino honors the Gerlingers at their anniversary celebration. Sheriff John Misterly is at right.

"You have built a business based on good business ethics, quality merchandise and uncompromising workmanship. Your business continues to be a credit to the community as various manufacturers depend upon you to help them pioneer many of the innovations in their respective industries. Consequently, it may be stated that you are also a credit to the motor-power industries and to our country."

Roy B. Ford
Aerojet-General Corporation

"I am frank to admit that I have much admiration for Gerlinger Motor Parts in that I feel that your company combines the better qualities to be found in any business enterprise...a policy founded upon the principles of mutual trust, integrity and loyalty."

C.W. Sawhill
Aeroquip Corporation

"You can be proud of the growth and progress of your company through the years, and the high esteem in which it is held. Such success is no accident. It is clearly the result of your own exceptional qualities, a tribute to your vision, judgment and leadership and especially to the integrity and high ethical standards for which you are so widely known and so well respected."

Ed Fink
Southern Pacific Company

"There is no substitute for the elemental virtues and qualities to which we allude when we speak of George and Ella Gerlinger. And there is no substitute for the commonplace qualities of truth, justice, courage, thrift, common sense and genuine sympathy with the feelings of others with whom you daily come in contact."

Daniel J. Hartnett
Automotive Service Industry
Association

"For a quarter of a century, Gerlinger Motor Parts, Inc. has enjoyed respect and admiration for its integrity, honesty and fair dealing with all who have had dealings or business association with it and the Board of Supervisors is pleased to recognize its outstanding reputation and to wish for it and its stockholders many more years of happy and successful operation.

Leslie E. Wood
Supervisor, Sacramento County

"On all occasions, and regardless of what my business has been, the Gerlingers have always given me the utmost in service and courtesy, even though some of the problems I presented to them were of an unusual nature requiring much knowledge and engineering skill...and I have always found Mr. Gerlinger more than willing to help out with these unusual problems—many times doing same without charge in order to help a person in trouble."

John Misterly
Sheriff, Sacramento County

Vice-mayor Phil Mering presents George Gerlinger with a plaque for his 25 years in business.

"There was a time I called your office on the phone and said 'I got a set of spark plugs at your place yesterday and three of them are bad. I want to bring them back.' George answered in a cheerful voice, 'That's all right, Lee, you don't need to bring them back. Your word is just as good as the spark plugs.' That's what we like: A fine, friendly attitude of interest and cooperation."

Lee Harrison
Sacramento Brick Company

"When a business remains in an ever-changing business community for a period of twenty-five years it has had to deserve the confidence of that community. Not only has Gerlinger Motor Parts held the confidence of its customers, it has grown with the area and has contributed in many ways to the betterment of Sacramento."

Al Eames
Al Eames Ford

"We take great pleasure in presenting your firm with the ASIA Distinguished Service Award. This award is given only to member firms who have been in business continuously for at least a quarter of a century. It not only acknowledges your firm's status as an 'industry old-timer,' but recognizes your constant service to the community and to the industry."

J.L. Wiggins
Executive Vice-president
Automotive Service Industry
Association

"The integrity and goodwill of your operation has been reflected in its increasing growth. Also the pleasant atmosphere in all departments indicates that your employees, too, are glad and proud to be a part of your organization."

Ray L. Chatfield
Bartalini and Hackett

But George had said his thank you's in other ways for 25 years—by paying strict attention to the needs of his customers, by his strong sense of responsibility and by his desire to deliver satisfaction.

By 1967, George and Ella Gerlinger were ready to retire. George's health had failed since he'd suffered a heart attack six years before. Besides, he'd worked since he'd been 15. It was time to relax and enjoy life—and to take advantage of the boats that still gave him so much pleasure.

In December of 1967, therefore, the controlling interest in Gerlinger Motor Parts was sold to Johnny Biggers, with the remaining stock divided among the five department heads: Paul Wilson, sales manager; Walt Beaty, shop foreman; Jim Hostetter, office manager; Frank Mencarini, manager of sales orders; and Larry Taxara, counter manager.

Leaving the bank that December day after signing the papers and documents, Johnny's feet barely touched the sidewalk. He smiled to himself as the words "John Biggers, President" flashed in his head like a neon sign.

He'd come a long way from the sickly little kid who wasn't supposed to live past his teenage years. He'd come a long way from his impoverished youth. With his faith in God and his loving wife and family to sustain him, he'd achieved the goal he'd set for himself when he was 17. He was owner of Gerlinger Motor Parts.

Vowing to uphold George Gerlinger's high standards and to protect the excellent reputation the firm had earned, Johnny suddenly remembered an old family saying that George liked to quote: "If you're not winning, you're losing. In business you're either going forward or you're sliding backwards. You can't be static."

John smiled again. He didn't plan to lose. He didn't plan to let Gerlinger's slide backwards or become static.

Jumping into his Cadillac, John turned toward K Street and another new beginning—a new beginning as owner and president of Gerlinger Motor Parts.

"One of the greatest talents of all is the ability to recognize talents in others."

Counter crew in 1965 included, from left, Frank Mencarini, Larry Taxara, Frank Sonier, Tom Ambrose and Dave Baker.

CHAPTER NINE

Of Despair and Determination

The night that fire engulfed Gerlinger Motor Parts and threatened to turn Johnny's dreams into ashes was one of the bleakest in his life.

Watching the turbulent orange flames blaze into the smouldering black sky, hearing the bomb-like explosions of pressurized cans and smelling the stench of burning acids, Johnny felt that everything he'd worked for was going up in smoke. Through stinging, bloodshot eyes, he gazed at the 15 to 20 fire trucks, the 60 firemen and the bright yellow ambulance filling the street in front of Gerlinger's and his heart sunk.

He couldn't believe there was that much to burn. The walls were cement. The walls in the rear were sheet metal. The equipment was steel. Nonetheless, the building was burning as if it were tinder.

Suddenly, Johnny was aware of a tugging on his sleeve and looked down to see Ella Gerlinger standing next to him, grasping at his coat. Misery was etched on her face as she faced the inferno that had been her dream too. Fighting to keep her poise, she began bombarding Johnny with her questions and her fears.

"Johnny, are your men with you? Will you reopen? Will you build here again? Will we all lose our investments? I lost George three years ago, will I lose this, too?"

Determined to maintain his equilibrium, Johnny stared at the woman. She'd known him almost all his life. She should know his love for the business. She should know that he'd never give up.

"We have insurance, Ella. You will be paid. I will not let Gerlinger's fail. Do you hear me? I will never let it fail."

Leaving Ella standing on the sidewalk, John reached into his pocket for his keys, pushed through the crowd and fumbled with the lock on the front door. Firemen, who had broken the window and were quickly feeding a hose through the jagged glass, stopped their task to intercept him.

"Hey, buddy. Get away from here. This place could blow any minute."

As if in a trance, John pushed the fireman away. "This is my business. I must go inside."

A strong arm encircled John's shoulders and he turned to see the sympathetic face of his friend, William Powell, Sacramento's fire chief.

"John, I'm sorry. I see fires every day, but this one really gets to me."

John shrugged off the comforting arm of his friend. "Bill, I'm determined to go inside. Please don't let them stop me."

Bill searched the almost crazed eyes of his friend then turned to the battalion chief and took him aside.

"Take him in, chief. He'll realize within 10 seconds that he can't stay."

As predicted, Johnny got three or four feet inside the door and was inundated with such an acrid smell and with such intense heat and smoke that he could neither see nor breathe.

Coughing, Johnny walked once again to the street, where microphones and cameras were thrust in his face by local press and television reporters.

"What were your thoughts when you first saw the fire, Mr. Biggers?"

"How much do you estimate you have lost?"

"Mr. Biggers, will you rebuild?"

Johnny answered in a daze, estimating the loss at more than $750,000 and assuring all who asked that he would rebuild. He pushed the aggressive newsmen away and turned toward a group of people huddled together across the street. His employees. They had seen reports of the fire on the nightly news and had one by one hurried to the scene.

One quick-thinking employee, Lonnie Lunsford, had jumped into a company truck and had driven to several all-night grocery stores, arriving back on the scene with dozens of boxes of baking soda to neutralize the battery acid that was attacking the firefighters and their clothing. As Johnny and the others watched, the firemen gratefully grabbed the yellow Arm and Hammer boxes and began spreading it on the acid, oil, water and debris that covered the 12,000 sq. ft. floor.

In the meantime, Frank Mencarini and several others had taken another company vehicle and had driven to the warehouse on 20th Street, bringing back a truck load of a "floor dry" product, made from rice hull by-products burned to an ash. The firemen immediately poured the ash on the floor and down the aisles, pleased that employees of the burning business were interested in their safety.

Johnny turned away from the scene in time to see Esther rushing toward him. He held out his arms to her, and the two of them hugged one another and cried. Still holding one another, they turned to face their employees. Many had tears streaming down their faces as well.

"John, what are we going to do?"

Moving their glance from one person to another, John and Esther attempted to assure the men and women gathered there. Johnny squeezed one man's hand, clapped another on the shoulder, smiled at still another while Esther quietly spoke to each of them in turn.

"Friends, none of you will lose one dime as a result of this fire," John told his loyal crew. "Until I run out of money myself, you'll each receive your paychecks. Now go home and get some rest. I want all of you back here at 8 tomorrow morning. We've got work

"You can tell the stature of a man by what it takes to get him upset."

to do."

Overcome with emotion, Johnny sent Esther home, too, then turned back to the scene of the now controlled fire. The roar of flames and the scream of sirens had been replaced with the eerie sounds of water dripping and trickling from still steaming rafters and the caved-in roof. As a uniformed security officer took his place in front of the smoldering ruins, Johnny realized there was nothing more he could do that night. Heading for his car, he was surprised to see Bill Hansen, the owner of Bearing Supply, approaching him.

"John, may I talk to you a minute?"

His face haggard and his body nearly dropping from exhaustion, John stopped and listened to the man who ran a competing and highly successful motor parts store on nearby L Street.

"John, I can't tell you how sorry I am about this . . .My wife and I just want to let you know that we'd be glad to loan you up to $100,000 to rebuild. No interest, either, until you're back on your feet."

John stared at the other man, unable to speak for a moment. He shook his head and felt new tears sting his eyes.

"But, why? Why would you make such an offer? We're competitors, remember?"

Bill Hansen put his arm around John's shoulder. "You're good, clean competition, John. I don't want to see you go broke. Sacramento needs you. It needs both of us."

Fire threatened Johnny's dream as it swept through Gerlinger Motor Parts.

Overwhelmed by the generosity and caring he'd encountered in the face of such tragedy, John thanked Bill and hurried to his car. All he wanted now was the solace of his wife and family.

The next morning, after a sleepless night, John and his employees arrived at 2020 K Street to survey the damage.

The fire that had caused such destruction the night before had been caused by an electrical malfunction. The failure of an automatic shutdown device caused a spark to arc and ignite the cooling oil in a rectifier in the plating department and to shoot a steam of burning oil through the walls between the store and the machine shop. The fire burned for 30 to 45 minutes before it burst through the roof and was spotted by neighbors. Exploding chemicals had sent fireballs across the building. So much "smog and fog" filled the machine shop that the air compressor was saturated with water and had filled the combustion chamber. The heads had been blown off the compressors from moisture in the air.

Surveying the damage, Johnny saw now that the chrome shop was completely demolished, as were the offices and the majority of the inventory. What didn't get ruined from the actual fire was ravaged from acid, fumes or heat. And, though he was covered by business interruption insurance, Johnny knew his coverage on the building and inventory fell short of his loss. But he'd worry about that later. Now he had to salvage what he could.

John's 35 employees were put to work immediately, spraying a total of 10 gallons of WD-40 over the smoke damaged machines to retard any further corrosion.

Defying police and fire officials who tried to order him off the premises, Johnny was determined to conduct business in the best way he could. Counter manager Lonnie Lunsford was placed in charge of moving salvageable supplies to the warehouse, where he was instructed to spend what he needed to set up a makeshift store. Within an hour, Lonnie had built a counter from sheets of plywood laid atop a foundation of Prestone Anti-Freeze cases. Meanwhile, Johnny had appealed to the top executive of the phone company and had persuaded him to send his repair crews to install temporary phones so that he could begin contacting customers and suppliers.

Within 12 hours of the fire that should have destroyed his $1.5 million-a-year enterprise, Johnny Bigger's was once again open for business.

"I've been involved in firefighting for over 20 years," says Fire Chief Bill Powell. "During that period of time, I have never seen a business back in operation in such a positive and professional manner."

Loyal customers, understanding suppliers and local businesses all rallied around the undefeatable Johnny Biggers and his company. They patiently waited at the improvised "counter" set up in the 3500-square-foot warehouse at 1114 20th St. while employees communicated via walkie-talkies to their fellow workers in the burned-out building who attempted to find supplies to service their faithful patrons. Purchasing agent Deane Prentice and counterman Bart Miller parked their C.B. radio-equipped vehicles nearby to aid the communications effort.

Long-time suppliers gave Gerlinger's a break by offering goods at discount, and Johnny and his team were elated that the Anco Company honored its policy of replacing their product line of windshield wiper arms and blades at no charge to any company losing Anco stock because of fire or flood. Other companies in the Sacramento area helped their fellow businessman by offering what they could.

"We have a shipping department. Would you like to use it until you can get back on your feet?"

"Do you need a truck? We have one we'd be glad to loan you."

"We have extra desks. Can you use them?"

"I have never seen a business, and specifically an owner, regroup his forces and put his business back in operation in such a positive and professional manner."

—*William R. Powell,*
Fire Chief
Sacramento Fire Department

"The unfortunate fire that occurred could have been fatal to a business that had less than top quality management."

—*E. Robert McDowall, President*
McDowall and Sons, Inc.

Next-door business neighbor, Fred Carnie, offered to share office space in his store, which had been saved from damage by a double concrete wall. However, tenants on the other side of the motor parts store had been planning a move anyway and offered to relocate early to accommodate the Gerlinger staff. Through the long winter months, Johnny and his workers fought the odds to keep the business alive. Luckily it was a dry and mild winter, for he and his employees worked under an open roof with no heat and very little light. Construction crews toiled around them and over their heads, but the dedicated men and women ignored the adversity and conducted their business "as usual."

Five months later, looking at the reconstruction that belied the recent devastation, Johnny took a deep sigh and mouthed a silent prayer of thanks. He had seen to it that all of his employees had maintained their jobs. He had managed to retain and serve all of his customers. And he had received the loyal support and help of the Sacramento business community.

Johnny smiled and once again reached for the letter he had received from John Misterly, the former sheriff of Sacramento County.

"Dear Johnny," the letter read. "Seems to me I remember telling you several years ago that unless you slowed down you would burn yourself out. Did not mean it the way it turned out. You sure did a remarkable job of recovery, but that's the Biggers way."

Johnny refolded the letter and replaced it in the desk of his newly-built office. Despite the tragic circumstances, he had felt truly blessed throughout the entire experience. The words of a well-loved and familiar hymn came to his mind and he found himself softly humming.

"He was there all the time," Johnny sang. "He was there all the time."

With the melody still reverberating in his head, John picked up the phone and began to dial. He had no more time for reflection or for looking backwards. His eyes were on the future, and it looked very promising, indeed.

"You sure did a remarkable job of recovery, but that's the Biggers' Way."

—John Misterly
Former Sheriff, Sacramento County

CHAPTER 10

From Motor Parts to Missiles

J ohn Biggers threw open the double doors of his motor parts store and greeted the group of students stepping off the Placerville school bus.

"Good morning, and welcome to Gerlinger's," he said as the high school automotive class gathered around him.

Scenes such as this were becoming more and more common at Gerlinger's, as John and his staff were frequently asked to open the machine shop to tours from local colleges and high schools.

Quickly walking the young men and women through the automotive retail and wholesale store and past the sales counter, John led the class through the side door and into the machine shop. Greeted by the resonating hum of compressors, the hissing of steam and the whooshing sounds of air being used as a power source throughout the shop, the students were wide-eyed as they observed the flurry of activity before them.

Technicians in neat blue uniforms were operating hundreds of thousands of dollars worth of shiny machines and equipment and, as the class members walked through the clean-swept aisles, their host described the machinery they were passing.

Turret lathes. Crankshaft grinders. A 15-foot long horizontal boring machine that could create perfectly aligned holes in the largest of engines. A magna-flux device that could discern the tiniest of cracks in metal. An 8-foot tall vertical boring machine that could be used to drill giant air compressor cylinders. Electronic testing units. A bead blasting machine that removed paint, surface particles and rust from equipment before it could be repaired.

As Johnny led the students through the shop, he stopped often to comment on a particular process and to answer questions.

Stopping in front of a huge $120,000 crankshaft grinder, he pointed out the 1000-pound roller being ground to rigid specifications on the device.

"The huge roller you see here is used by the Campbell Company to prepare noodles for the soups your mothers cook you for lunch," Johnny told the class. "Our hard chrome plating capabilities and our advanced techniques have brought us a lot of business from the food processing industry."

Johnny went on to tell the students of the time he was asked to put his skills to work for Chef Boy-ar-dee. "It seems that the roller

"I never needed competition to excel."

bar that formed the ravioli would quickly wear down to the point that the pasta it formed was too thin," Johnny said, going on to explain that he and his staff had created a technique for building up the webbing of the roller head so that the thickness of the ravioli would consistently meet the food processing company's specifications.

Continuing on the tour, Johnny pointed out other jobs in various stages of repair. A 100-inch crankshaft for a semitractor, a huge rail car air conditioner, funneling equipment used to fill frozen dinners and skimming devices with large impellers to clean up offshore oil spills. Moving even further into the shop, Johnny pointed to equipment from a New York City sewage plant and a giant screw-like device for use in preparing pizza dough.

"One of the most exciting jobs we've had recently was rebuilding the giant engine of a stand-by generator used by McClellan Air Force Base," said Johnny.

The students listened intently as Johnny explained how machinists Bob Scott and Mike Morisette had stripped the 7000-pound engine block from the 15-foot long, 10-foot tall generator with the aid of an 8000-pound forklift.

"They brought it back here to the shop, stripped it of its paint and removed the cylinder sleeves, then installed new sleeves and rebuilt all the accessories, including fuel pumps, oil and water pumps and the turbo charger," said Johnny. "Then they completely cleaned all the parts, painted them and took them back to the base where they reassembled the generator. It was a three-month, $100,000 project and the largest engine we had done to date."

Biggers Industrial Gerlinger rebuilds all kinds of engines,

"The bitterness of poor quality remains long after the sweetness of low price is forgotten."

Mike Morisette was instrumental in rebuilding the stand-by generator used by McClellan Air Force Base.

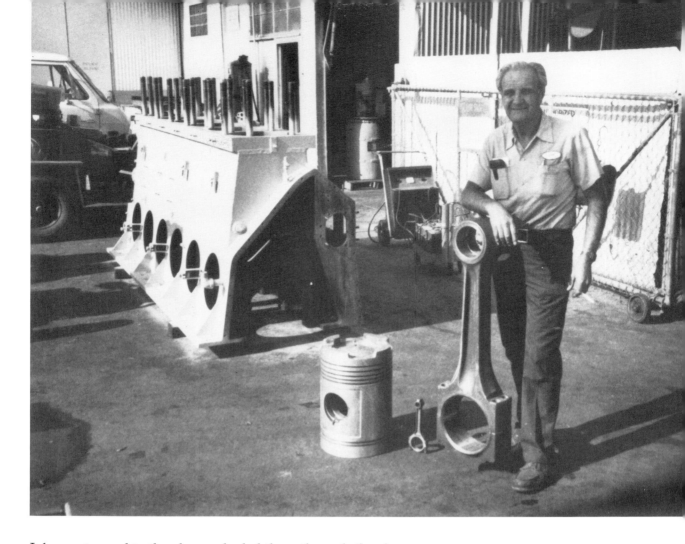

Johnny stressed to the class as he led them through the shop.

"Most of the automotive engines we work on are of American design," he said, "but for more than four decades now we've gained a reputation for the rebuilding of Rolls Royce engines. In fact we recently rebuilt the engine from a Silver Cloud owned by Bob Cottam, president of the Rolls Royce Club of America."

After showing the automotive class through both the high tech and mechanical sections of the plant, Johnny walked them back to the front of the store and saw them back onto their bus.

He waved as the large yellow vehicle pulled into traffic and then walked back inside, reflecting on the tour and how it made him so aware of the vast changes that had taken place at Gerlinger's during his career.

I wouldn't change a day of the last 42 years, he thought to himself, not even a day.

John Biggers admits his years with the company have been so exciting because he's constantly searching for new challenges. In 1967 when he took ownership of the company, he set his sights on continuing and expanding the industrial trend of the business. Like George Gerlinger before him, John insisted on meeting precision standards for both the automotive and industrial needs of his customers. Every piece of equipment in the shop was regulated to

Shop Foreman Jim McBride leans on a connecting rod from a Baldwin engine, used by the USAF and rebuilt in the Gerlinger shop. For comparison, the smaller rod, to the left, is from a three-ton GMC truck.

.0001 of an inch.

"You could take a single hair from my head and slice it 36 times—that's how accurate it is," John likes to explain.

This high-precision equipment has made it easy for him to set his sights high. And the sky has been the limit. Literally. Every space flight, from the first sub-orbital mission to the recent journeys of the space shuttles, has carried hardware fashioned in the Sacramento shop. The artisans at Gerlingers still speak with excitement as they remember the role they've played in the nation's space program. The lunar probes, Alan Shephard's momentous journey into the heavens and John Glenn's historic orbit of the earth are all sources of pride for the Gerlinger crew, as are the more recent missions.

John still laughs when he remembers Glenn's last words as he climbed aboard *Friendship 7*. "Just think," the astronaut said, "this giant bird was put together by the lowest bidder."

Being the lowest bidder allowed the Biggers Industrial Division of Gerlinger's to take part in a variety of other exciting ventures also—undertakings that have led the company into the nation's past as well as its future.

On display in the Railroad Museum in Sacramento today is the famed *C.P. Huntington*, the steam engine that made the chronicled trip that linked the east and west when the golden spike was driven

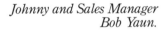

Johnny and Sales Manager Bob Yaun.

The machine shop at 2020 K Street.

"John is able to do routinely what others are afraid to attempt."

—*Robert N. Cottam*
G.W. Williams Co.

into the transcontinental railway in Promontory, Utah, in 1869. Parts for the venerable locomotive were refurbished in the Gerlinger machine shop, allowing the company once again to participate in a project linked to America's history.

And when the Olympics were staged in Los Angeles in 1984, Biggers Industrial had a hand in those unforgettable Summer Games as well when the company was asked to design, assemble and build a VIP Power Car for Southern Pacific Railroad.

"Southern Pacific wanted to position dining and lounge cars on the tracks for use by heads of state, corporate executives and Olympic officials," explains Johnny. "But they didn't want to leave a 4000 horsepower locomotive engine on the tracks to supply the energy needs of the VIP cars."

Mike Morisette was assigned as project engineer on the eight-month job and was involved in all phases of the construction, from conceptionalizing the design to the finished product.

Biggers Industrial Gerlinger designed, assembled and built the VIP Power Car Southern Pacific Railroad used during the 1985 Summer Olympics.

"I basically have an automotive background," says Mike, "but I love to be continually challenged. The Power Car project was really exciting and was on my mind constantly. We were being asked to create something that had never been done before. I was so involved in the project that I even dreamed about it."

The assignment of Biggers Industrial, according to Mike, was to strip a 70-foot baggage car and equip it with 60,000 pounds of equipment, including a 175 KW diesel generator, a boiler with the capacity to produce 30,000,000 BTUs of steam daily, a water storage and softening system and sound muffling insulation. The power car was also equipped with an automatic Halon gas fire suppression system, says Mike. In short, the car was designed to supply all the heat, steam, electricity, treated water and air conditioning needs of six to sixteen dining and lounge cars, freeing the locomotive to do the job for which it was intended—pulling trains around the country.

Biggers Industrial was involved in the construction of the power car for almost a year, working with 25 experts in remote circuitry, electronics, pneudraulics, safety design and explosion-proofing. It was a project John thoroughly enjoyed. Despite the fact that Gerlinger MPI/Biggers Industrial has no research department, conceptualizing such designs and problem solving are among

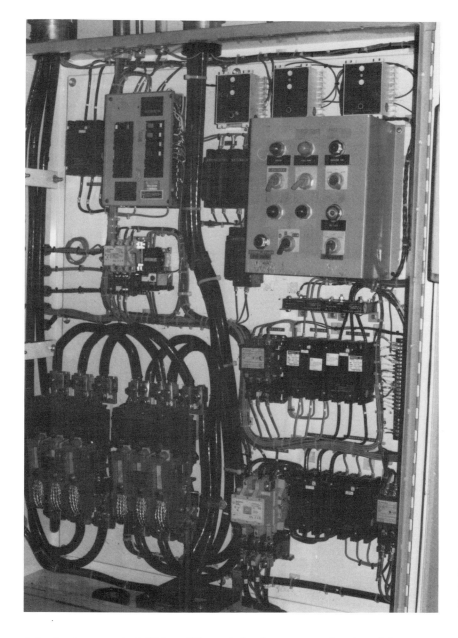

Controls for the VIP Power Car involved complicated circuitry.

John's strongest abilities. Though he has no professional degrees hanging on his office wall, he considers himself "a practical engineer" because of his long years of experience.

He also enjoys troubleshooting.

"If someone tells me something can't be done, that's like saying 'sic 'em' to a dog," he jokes. Bob Davidson, who owns Davidson Press in Sacramento, is quite aware of John's tenacity and dedication. He remembers a time when one of his presses "seized up" and refused to budge.

"I called John, who immediately sent over his head machinist, Jim McBride," says Davidson. "It took Gerlinger's half the time to fix the press that it would have taken the manufacturer."

Others agree.

"John Biggers is the embodiment of the American Dream. He's standing at the top of the staircase now, but he climbed every step. He didn't take an elevator."

—Anneliese Heimburg
Retired Assistant Office
Manager
Gerlinger MPI/Biggers
Industrial

"Our request to resurface and hard chrome 12 rollers was handled both promptly and professionally," says William Jackson, district supervisor for the Kodak Company. "The two-week turn-around time allowed us to expeditiously fulfill our obligations to our customer. In fact, the resurfaced rollers are performing spectacularly." John Goncalves, retired quality control supervisor and foreman for Southern Pacific, says he knew he could always depend on Gerlinger's.

"If I kept all the railroad's equipment running, I was doing my job," says Goncalves, "and if I was in dire need, I'd get in touch with John Biggers himself."

The former railroad man remembers a time when one of his Jim Bean steam turbines needed graphite seals. The parts seemed impossible to find for the outdated turbine model, but Johnny wouldn't give up.

"He called all over the country," remembers Goncalves. "It took him a month, but he got the parts I needed."

There was a time, however, when the Gerlinger Company didn't quite live up to its reputation, the former Southern Pacific employee says with a chuckle.

"Once Gerlinger's promised that a cone for our boring machines would be ready by the end of the day, so I told my boss that the machine would be in operation at that time. Something went wrong, and the cone was not ready when I went to pick it up, and I got so mad that I 'fired' the entire Gerlinger crew."

When Johnny found out what happened, he kept his machinists on overnight to perfect the cone.

"It was ready for me the next morning," says Goncalves, "so I rehired all of the men I'd fired!"

John Biggers dedication to his customers, his strict attention to detail and the sophistication of his machine work have won him a reputation that is unequaled.

He is described by his customers and fellow businessmen as a progressive leader and a sharp entrepreneur who is firm, fair and honest as well as caring, courteous and helpful.

"No one adjective can describe Johnny Biggers," says Stephen E. Alstrolm, purchasing agent for Sacramento Foods, Inc. "He is one of the kindest, most polite professionals with whom I have ever dealt. No matter how busy, John has always taken the time to help."

"He has a fine personality and the unique ability of always making his customers feel wanted and welcomed," adds Gordon K. Van Vleck, Secretary for Resources with the State of California.

"And John will always be able to relate to the common, ordinary person because he remembers his own humble beginnings," explains Bob Foster, director of personnel and employee relations at Computer Sciences Corporation.

Among his varied clients are Amtrak, Bay Area Rapid Transit, Campbell Soup, American Foods, Aerojet, McDonnell-Douglas Astronautics, Pacific Gas and Electric, the Sacramento Municipal Utility District and the United States Navy and Air Force. In addition, Gerlinger MPI/Biggers Industrial has done extensive work for lumber mills in the Northern California area, has sold materials to Folsom Dam and has contracts with five national railroads because of the company's involvement in hydraulics and unit rebuilding for heavy equipment.

It is obvious that John Biggers stands tall in the business world of Sacramento and northern California, and it is equally apparent that his sights are set on an increasing national and international market as well.

"I'm not one to look over my shoulder," he explains. "I prefer to look forward to the challenges ahead."

*John Biggers with General
Earl T. O'Loughlin,
Commander of the USAF.*

CHAPTER ELEVEN

A Man of Commitment

Is it the TRUTH?
Is it FAIR to all concerned?
Will it build GOODWILL and BETTER FRIENDSHIPS?
Will it be BENEFICIAL to all concerned?

This Rotary Four Way Test, the credo of Rotarians world-wide, is a doctrine taken very seriously by John Biggers. In dealings with his family, with members of his church and his community and with clients and competitors, John Biggers applies the principles of the international service club to his life.

"Johnny Biggers is a role model—the kind of person you like being around," says Scott Mize, the director of development for Jesuit High School in Sacramento who is also a retired colonel and former director of personnel at McClellan Air Force Base. "He's bright, sensitive and in touch with himself and his God. He has a great zest for life and seeks opportunities to make people feel good about themselves and their achievements."

"And success seems to make him more aware of the little guy or those less fortunate," adds Judge John M. Bodley.

John Biggers is held in high esteem in the Sacramento community and is described as a "doer" in the truest sense of the word. A civic leader who sits on the boards and advisory councils of dozens of city and county organizations and committees, he believes in giving something back to the community that has been so good to him.

Throughout the years he has been active in trade organizations within the automotive industry and has volunteered his time to the Boy Scouts, the Sacramento Safety Council, the Crime Alert Board, the Chamber of Commerce and numerous other civic and charitable groups.

Johnny's gift of giving began when he was a teenager and began volunteering his time by leading the congregational singing at his church. Always a music lover, John was a natural choice when Pastor Clyde Casto needed a music conductor for his Youth for Christ rallies. Later, when the North Area Ministerial Association was looking for someone to stimulate more interfaith activity among

At the annual Safety Council Meeting, John visits with County Supervisor Toby Johnson.

fundamental churches, Johnny was chosen to lead the music in a monthly "Singspiration," and enjoyed that position for more than 20 years—first on an interdenominational basis and then for the 13 Nazarene churches in the Sacramento district.

"John Biggers is a principled person who applies those principles to the totality of life. He is unashamedly and aggressively Christian and demonstrates in a significant way that a person can live by Christian principles and not merely survive but succeed in the tough business world."

—Jim Bond
President
Point Loma Nazarene College

During the 50th anniversary celebration of McClellan Air Force Base, John met with Major General Jim Wahleithner, below, and Colonel Bob Haines, director of the ALC personnel at McClellan Air Force Base, bottom.

His love of "making a joyful noise unto the Lord" has given him the opportunity to sing with such notables as Ethel Waters, Roy McKeon, Cliff Barrows and Rex Humbard. And, probably the most exciting moment in his musical career was leading the singing before thousands of people in the Sacramento Memorial Auditorium during a pre-Billy Graham crusade rally held there.

Johnny's love of music has led him to inspire others as well, including Ron "Jeff" Jeffries, song evangelist for the Church of the Nazarene.

"In 1953 our family arrived in Sacramento as the parsonage family of North Sacramento Nazarene Church," says Jeff. "Johnny was the first person we talked to and the first to welcome us. He became my Sunday School teacher, my friend and my advisor when I had a teenage problem. He is the man I learned more from about church congregational song leading than any college professor I later had—and the man, other than my father, that I wanted to grow up to be like. I have loved and appreciated Johnny over the years for his faithfulness to God and Christian ideals, for his fairness in all situations, for his great sense of humor and attitude toward life, and most of all for his friendship and Christian example that has helped me in so many situations for all these years. I wouldn't be doing what I am today if it wasn't for his early influence on my music career."

Johnny's influence has spread farther than just the Sacramento area. It has been felt worldwide. Ken Staniforth, a minister in the Church of the Nazarene, distinctly remembers how John affected his early days as a pastor serving abroad.

"My first pastoral assignment with the denomination was a difficult one in the heart of London," recalls Ken. "Things were sometimes discouraging and often, after taking the children to school, I would walk across Clapham Common, inwardly bewailing my lot and praying that the Lord would somehow spirit me away to some easier place.

"One Sunday the Biggers entered our lives unexpectedly and briefly. The day had not been a memorable one from our point of view and my wife and I were prepared to retire early. We donned our night attire and then the phone rang. An American voice answered. It was a Christian business man who was in England on a short visit and he wished to speak to a British pastor before he went home. We dressed quickly and waited for the mystery man.

"A large London taxi drew up outside and within a few seconds we were whisked into the presence of the cabby, who Johnny introduced to us as though he had been his friend for life. No time for British stiff upper lip protocol! He asked the taxi driver to wait while he had a chat with us.

"Inside the parsonage the Biggers testified of their saving relationship with Christ, spoke of the history of Gerlinger's and, most impressive of all, shared how God had been made a partner in the business. After a prayer, our twenty minute meeting was over, and the black Austin disappeared into the chilly London night, leaving with us impressions that lingered on through subsequent years of ministry in my metropolitan parish.

"It was as though a fresh breeze had blown across our lives. Our spirits had been lifted in a time of need. We had been introduced to a rare breed of person—a human dynamo with a flair for business who was also one of Christ's gentlemen. I had read about, but had never met until that night, anyone that had put God first in his business. Enthusiasm is contagious and, on that Sunday evening, I caught a little and was encouraged "

Johnny's and Esther's missionary work has also taken them to Central and South America. Along with Shirley Gale, Marge Atwood and Janie and Stan DeBoard, the couple attended the dedication of a church that the North Church of the Nazarene had funded in Chenendago, Nicaragua. Later, they took another missionary trip to Colombia and Peru and spent a week with their

"Paul, the Apostle, studied under teachers who were world renowned and was educated and carefully schooled in the high ranking society of the day. After he became an apostle, he chose to become one of the most effective followers of Christ of all time. I'm inspired by his example."

Johnny and Esther share many happy moments.

good friends, Bob and Maunette Gray, mission directors of Peru. On the same trip, they visited Brazil, meeting missionaries James and Carolyn Kratz and traveling 10,000 miles with them throughout the largest South American country.

Of course, Johnny serves his church with more than his singing voice and his missionary zeal. He offers his business and professional expertise on myriad committees and boards and, according to Pastor Bill Porter, is one of the pillars of the Nazarene Church.

"He's one of the most valued consultants we have," says Porter. "He has an awareness of the past, a sense of the present and a vision for the future."

John's devotion to his church, combined with the long hours he spent at Gerlinger's, kept him very occupied during the early years of his career. However, by the mid-50s, he decided that he'd like to take a more active role in community affairs.

"Sacramento had been very good to me," explains John, "and I wanted to do something to repay that goodness. Also, I have always believed that one person could make a difference, and I wanted to become involved in making a change for the good."

Despite his good intentions, John wasn't sure how to go about becoming "a mover and a shaker," and his humble beginnings had not prepared him for meeting the influential people in his community.

His chance came during the 1950s when he met Willard E. Nielsen, the city's former vice-mayor.

"I was calling on local businesses on behalf of the United Crusade," remembers Nielson, "and John eagerly responded. He understood the fact that I was donating my time, but beyond that wanted to know how he and his company could get involved in the community."

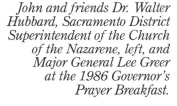

John and friends Dr. Walter Hubbard, Sacramento District Superintendent of the Church of the Nazarene, left, and Major General Lee Greer at the 1986 Governor's Prayer Breakfast.

Nielsen suggested that Johnny become active in a local charity or the Boy Scouts.

"This he did," says the former vice-mayor. "And look at him now."

Look at him now, indeed. John's listings in *Who's Who in America, Who's Who in the World* and other such publications take column inch after column inch to record his accomplishments and contributions and attest to the age-old adage that if you want something done, ask the busiest man you can find. And, while he's still not met any kings or emperors, he's touched shoulders with four presidents as well as with state and federal governmental officials, world-acclaimed movie stars and exciting sports figures.

"Mr. Biggers is one of the most able community leaders I have had the good fortune to know..."

— *Toby Johnson*
Supervisor, Fifth District

"For any worthy cause you can count on John," says Frank Corti, owner of the Corti Brothers supermarkets in the Sacramento area. "Most give lip service to causes and projects but, when push comes to shove, you can't find them. But John is a person you can always count on."

Frank Corti and John are members of the Sacramento Rotary Club, the largest club of its kind in northern California and the twenty-first largest Rotary Club in the world. The two men also serve on the Board of Directors of the Safety Council and are deeply involved in Sacramento's "Safetyville," a child-sized village built to teach youngsters safety rules and respect for law and order. A showplace that has received nationwide publicity, Safetyville is visited by school children from eleven counties. A pintsized courthouse features mock trials and gives boys and girls a firsthand look at the American justice system.

"It's a positive and fun way to teach students to be good—and safe—citizens," says Johnny.

Among the celebrities Johnny enjoys knowing is race car driver Mario Andretti.

John's commitment to youth is well known. Though he never had the opportunity to attend college himself, he sits on committees and chairs meetings with college presidents and school superintendents throughout the Sacramento area. He is on the advisory councils of Sacramento City College and the Los Rios Community College District. In addition, he has chaired the automotive and vocational program and the all industries area-wide business and career division for Sacramento County Schools. Perhaps his deepest commitment is to the Sacramento Metro Industry Education Council (SMIEC), which he served as president for four years. Dedicated to preparing disadvantaged youth for job opportunities in business and industry, SMIEC was founded to find employment for youths before they run afoul of the law and become inmates of juvenile hall at taxpayers' expense.

A frequent lecturer for SMIEC workshops as well as for more conventional classrooms, Johnny speaks on the free enterprise system and on a Horatio Alger theme. Nattily dressed, the articulate

As president of the Sacramento Industry Education Council, Johnny worked with, from left, Rick Rodriguez, one of many who obtained employment through the council's youth project; Ed Prentice of ABC Supply Company, which supplied jobs for many project graduates; and Pat Dietler, the council's executive director.

"John Biggers is a man who is honorable, keeps his commitments and has a spirit of adventure. He tries to make his community a better place to live. He is one of the most unforgettable men I have ever met."

—Albert Rogers
President
Rogers Machine Co.

and self-assured John Biggers is proof to young people from all walks of life that the American Dream is alive and well.

"I'm proof to those kids that you don't have to be born with a silver spoon in your mouth to become successful," says Johnny, who enjoys sharing the story of his own impoverished childhood.

"I also like to joke with them that I was the first ROP student in the state," he says, referring to the highly regarded Regional Occupations Program in which students receive on-site training in the field of their choice. "They enjoy hearing how I began working full-time in the automotive business when I was 14."

John's lectures aren't limited to the young people of his community, however. Civic and service organizations as well as church groups are appreciative audiences as he spreads his upbeat philosophy. And, since the fire that almost obliterated his business, he has devoted much of his time to addressing others about fire protection and adequate insurance.

"John is a caring and dynamic man," says Al Howenstein, State Director of the Office of Criminal Justice Planning and a former Sheriff of Marin County. "He has boundless energy and a strong sense of community responsibility."

His enthusiasm and adherence to civic duty have earned Johnny dozens of letters of commendation, certificates of appreciation and resolutions from the city and county. Competing for space on his office wall, they hang as proud testaments to the important role and reputation he has earned as a leader in the Sacramento community.

"John is an entrepreneur who knows how to transform opportunity into action. A skilled negotiator and a man that approaches problems with a positive attitude. A fun person to be with.

—Robert C. Matin
Purchasing agent
Wemco

Of course, those who know Johnny well say that he has given much more than time, money and service to the community. He's also given the world the "Johnny Biggers Knife," they say with a smile. The shiny red pocketknife, with his company's logo on one side and his name on the other, has become almost a trademark.

Among Johnny's many friends is Brigadier General Frank Tidwell, formerly Vice-Commander ALC at McClellan Air Force Base.

John and Colonel Scott Mize, personnel director at McClellan, top, and with Don Howton, Director of Public Affairs, and Brigadier General Jim Hopp, below.

"Gerlinger's began handing out these knives as a promotional item in 1950," says Johnny, who remembers that they were a popular item with customers from the first day.

However, George Gerlinger didn't especially approve of knives as give-away items because of the superstitions attached to them.

"Supposedly a knife was never to be exposed between friends because it would cut the friendship, and George was afraid that people would associate our pocketknives with that superstition," says Johnny.

Just the opposite proved true, and today it is almost a status symbol to be carrying a "Johnny Biggers Knife" in pocket or purse. Johnny hands out between 500 and 1000 of the knives each year to new accounts, to those who make large purchases and to dignitaries of cities, states and the federal government.

Among those carrying the surgical steel knife are Ronald Reagan and his wife Nancy, evangelist Billy Graham, actors Lorne Greene and Jane Fonda, sports stars Hank Aaron, Willie Mays and Billy Martin, Mario Andretti, Major General Dewey Lowe, George Deukmejian and the previous four governors of California and about 40 heads of state, according to Johnny.

Used prosaically as letter openers, nail files and for opening packages, the knives have been reported to have had more unusual uses also.

"I've heard of one doctor who's used his knife to perform an emergency tracheotomy," says Johnny, "and another doctor friend of mine used his to skin a kangaroo when he was in Australia, and Bill Scanlon, the former State Director of the Department of Motor Vehicles uses his for 'surgery' on his game birds."

"I know John Biggers as a predictable, non-changing person. He is predictably always pleasant and warm-hearted."

—Vern Nelson
Drugless Therapist

Whether he's handing out knives or business advice and whether he's leading a churchful of singers or a committee of company executives, Johnny's management skills are evident.

"I've been told that I handle people well," he admits, "and I credit the Bible with teaching me how.

Secretary of the US Air Force Vern Orr, at left, meets with John and Major General Dewey K.K. Lowe, former ALC Commander at McClellan Air Force Base.

"For example," he says, "when the children of Israel were on their way to Canaan, they were very hesitant about going, so God placed swarms of bees behind them to speed them on their way."

And just how does Johnny translate this persuasive tactic into modern life? As an example, he relates a story concerning the very narrow parking lot on K Street, where he had to leave his car every day. It seems that one unthinking driver never pulled his car into his space far enough, which made it difficult for others to squeeze past as they drove down the row. At first, Johnny left notes on the car's windshield telling the owner that it would make it easier for others if he would pull his vehicle as far forward into the space as possible. When he got no response to his polite request, Johnny decided to use "a swarm of bees."

"I left a note on his car the next day that said, 'I'm sorry I smacked your bumper as I drove past. If you had pulled farther forward, this wouldn't have happened.'"

In truth, Johnny had smacked the bumper—with his hand— and, from that day on, the car was parked correctly, he reports with a wide smile.

ALC Commander Major General Lee V. Greer and Shirley O'Loughlin, wife of General Earl O'Loughlin, join Johnny and Esther at one of Sacramento's social events.

This good-natured sense of fairness has not only made John Biggers an excellent citizen but a well-loved and respected employer as well. According to Anneliese Heimburg, a retired employee who served Gerlinger's for 25 years, the company was like a second family.

"Mr. Gerlinger was almost a father figure and Mr. Biggers a big brother," she says. "They provided the necessary authority but there was also concerned and loving guidance."

One thing that set Johnny apart from other employers, Mrs. Heimburg continues, is that prayer meetings were held each morning before hours for any employee who wanted to participate.

"It was almost as if Jesus Christ were a silent partner in the business," she says.

Anneliese Heimburg also credits John Biggers with expanding the company's benefit program and with initiating a profit sharing plan, which she says was an excellent way to encourage employees to be even more dedicated and production-oriented.

"John Biggers serves as a wonderful example for all of us with his positive approach to life," she concludes. "He even took the devastation of the fire and turned it into a springboard for improvement. He's an inspiration and the embodiment of the American dream."

Johnny poses with, from left, Robert Cottam, president of Rolls Royce Club of America, and Pastor William Porter.

"John Biggers stands tall in the Sacramento business world."

—*Colonel John D. Wood*
Base Commander
McClellan Air Force Base

John, with my deepest personal regards,
Ronald Reagan

A friend of presidents, John Biggers received a photo from President Ronald Reagan and shakes hands with former president Richard M. Nixon during the 1960 election.

To John Biggers With best wishes,
Richard Nixon

"Sacramento is 'bigger and better' because of John Biggers!"

—Pat Dietler
Executive Director
SMIEC
and
John Dietler
State Dept. of Corrections

Perhaps one of the greatest illustrations of faith in Johnny as an employer came when, after 42 years of being members of the Teamsters and Machinists Unions, his employees decided they no longer wanted to be represented by Local 165 and Local 2182.

"When we suffered a fire and it looked like we might be wiped out, you took the loss and pain and led us out of what could have been a catastrophy," his employees explained. "We got paid for every hour we had coming. And, during business down-turns, you kept all of us on full pay. Neither union asked us if we needed them to work with us in any of those circumstances."

Some people might think that supporting a large family while working up to president of a successful company would be all a man could handle—as well as all he could hope to achieve. But those people haven't met John Biggers and haven't observed his zest for life.

"I just enjoy living," he shrugs when asked how he does it. "When I work, I work. When I play, I play. And when I get involved, I give it everything I've got."

Dr. Billy Graham visits the Rotary Club of Sacramento and meets, from left, Cal, Marlene, Johnny and Curt.

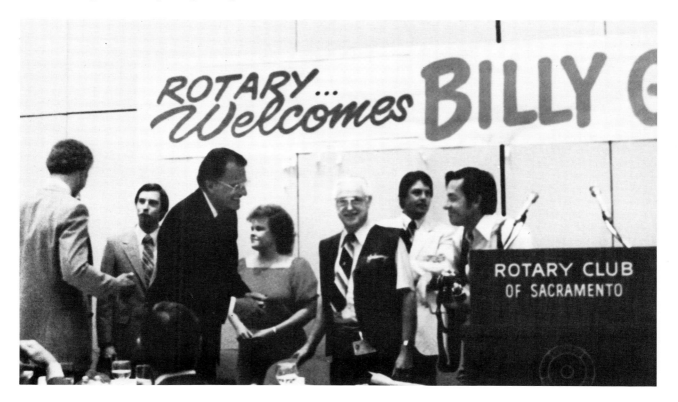

At play in Acapulco, Johnny caught a 9-ft., 1-in., 132-pound sailfish. The fish is still on display at Biggers Industrial Gerlinger.

CHAPTER TWELVE

New Paths

Forty years after Johnny Biggers left his childhood sickbed with the determination to burn out at a young age rather than rust out at 95, he again faced a crisis that would change his life.

Extreme tiredness, a lack of his characteristic vitality, and finally a fainting spell that left him breathless and disoriented were warning signs that led him once again to seek the services of a cardiac specialist.

"Doctor, I just don't understand what's wrong with me. I've always burned the candle at both ends, so to speak, but usually the more jobs and commitments I undertake the more energy I have for the next project that comes along. I don't know why that's changed so in the last few months."

Johnny sat in the office of Dr. Robert Allen and waited for an answer from the prominent Sacramento physician.

"John, the heart, like any other organ, requires energy and oxygen to perform its work. And it depends on a system of arteries to provide that energy and oxygen."

The doctor rose and walked to the large heart diagram hanging on the wall and pointed out John's problem areas.

"The arteries in your heart are severely blocked. If you want to live to celebrate Christmas this year, my recommendation is immediate surgery."

With the love and support of his family and friends and the prayers of his pastor, his congregation and Nazarene missionaries worldwide, as well as the warm wishes of his business associates, John Biggers entered Mercy General Hospital to undergo openheart surgery in October 1982. He knew that his heart would be stopped and removed from his chest for the procedure, but Johnny was bolstered by his faith and the love surrounding him.

Just before being given the anesthetic, Johnny grasped Dr. Allen's hand. "Doctor, I rebuild engines and sometimes, even though we do all the right things, the engine just won't start. I hope the same thing doesn't happen with heart specialists."

Smiling and marveling that his patient could respond to the situation with such a sense of humor, the doctor assured Johnny that he expected the operation to be a great success and that it would offer him a new lease on life.

And it did.

Recovering from his ordeal on the day after the surgery, John was amused to read about himself in Kirt MacBride's column in the Sacramento Bee.

"It looks as though John Biggers has the distinction of having been operated on for more bypasses at one time than anyone since surgeons began bypassing at Mercy...Seven! He's recovering nicely."

Johnny's recuperation was brightened by the hundreds of cards and letters he received and by the dozens upon dozens of plants and flower arrangements that were delivered to his room. Esther and Marlene attached ribbon streamers to the walls and taped more than 300 get-well cards to them.

"There was standing room only for the flowers," remembers Marlene, "and nurses would stop by each day to take a look at Dad's display."

During the 28 days that John was hospitalized, he lay in his bed with his mind racing.

"It was if I were re-energized," Johnny remembers. "I guess my brain had been starved for oxygen before the surgery, but now it was going 300 miles an hour. The only problem was that my feet were still on the bed."

He realized that he'd been given yet another opportunity at life—and he realized that new life could no longer resemble a treadmill. The shop was running quite efficiently without him. Calvin had joined the company more than a year before as secretary-treasurer and Curt had come on board as vice-president of sales and marketing the month before John had entered the hospital. They, along with Frank Mencarini, vice-president of sales orders; Jim McBride, shop foreman; and Don Henderson, counter manager, were doing a superb job. Their committed efforts and sense of teamwork as well as their tribunal system of making decisions kept the business operating smoothly.

Johnny knew it was time to step back from Gerlinger's. But he also knew he needed a place to step to.

"I've never seen anyone with such a positive response to recuperation," says family pastor Bill Porter. "There was never any doubt that he would get better. But he knew that he'd have to slow down. He took a course in cardiac care and then concentrated on making his hospital time creative time."

Johnny first decided to use his revitalized energy by learning to operate a computer.

"I thought I'd be able to use all my brain power and not have to go anywhere," he says. "But I got bored fast."

As if by providential design, Johnny received a video camera for Christmas that year. He'd always enjoyed photography and was familiar with editing techniques from taking home movies of his children when they were small. What's more, the video equipment utilized the new computer technology that he'd just learned and gave him a creative way to spend his recuperating hours. The doctor was only allowing him to work partime at the shop, so each afternoon he would devote his unflagging energies to learning all he could about the capabilities of his "new toy."

Just before his surgery, John and Esther had hired a construc-

Nola Joy Carello, Sacramento television producer and talk show host, and Johnny, in his capacity of president of the Safetyville 200 Club, starred in a public service announcement on bicycle safety. Besides Johnny's granddaughter, Julie, on bicycle, other children include, from left, Kevin Bracy, Tonya Hale, Brian Fernando, Julie Holmes, Sandra Fernando and Donald Fox.

tion crew to add two new rooms to their home—a master bedroom and an office. However, now Johnny decided that the new addition would make a perfect video studio.

"At first I thought I'd use the camera solely to record family events," says John, "but in no time at all people were asking me to videotape their weddings and other special events—I was even asked to film a funeral."

Within two months, Johnny had bought a second camera as well as a professional video camera and was renting his equipment to a local photographer. Soon he was taping governmental affairs at the Capitol, such as the State of the State Address and other newsworthy events.

"I've never really liked the programming on conventional television," he admits, "so I thought the videos I was producing could fill a void."

It wasn't long before he decided a travelogue would make interesting entertainment and made arrangements to do a videotape of the Yosemite Valley.

By March 1983 Johnny's "hobby" had outgrown his home video room, and he rented office space at the savings and loan building around the corner from Gerlinger's. He was introduced to Ted Langdell, a talented young man with a background in radio and television and an affinity for taping and producing quality videos.

A flurry of activity followed, and Johnny, who had been looking for a diversion not a new career, found himself busier than ever fulfilling his new video commitments.

He and Ted taped legislative arguments on important bills in the assembly and senate and sold them to television stations throughout California. John's friend, Jim Keever, was reunited with his mother after 40 years and asked Johnny to record the happy, yet tearful event. The resulting clip was shown on television stations in

California and Oregon. Another friend, John Sullivan, retired from Trailways after completing 2,000,000 accident-free miles in his bus driving career—a feat that Johnny captured on tape and which was again shown on television news stations in California and Oregon.

Within weeks, the Sacramento Safety Council, the Sacramento Metropolitan Industry Education Council, development companies and other businesses in the area were knocking on Johnny's new door, wanting him to tape advertisements and public service announcements. Outgrowing the one office he rented from the savings and loan, Johnny added another four more rooms to his lease and expanded his video company accordingly.

With his keen business sense, Johnny realized quickly that if his new enterprise was to be successful he would need to form a partnership to fund the growing firm. Prices of the state of the art equipment he required were prohibitive. One camera set-up with its ancillary equipment came with a sales tag of $40,000, editing equipment was good for another $50,000 and character generators, audio boards and other equipment necessary for a quality product cost tens of thousands of dollars more.

JBVP Video Studios boasts some of the industry's most sophisticated electronic equipment and cameras, such as the 600-line broadcast quality camera shown above. Ted Langdell and Merlene Biggers Mencarini at work in the JBVP Studios.

In January 1984, just 15 months after his open heart surgery, Johnny Biggers Video Productions was officially born. The new enterprise had grown from one small office to two—and then to an entire complex of offices. Pam Baker was hired as music coordinator, Marilyn Morin as marketing manager, Merlene Mencarini as office manager, Ted Langdell to head production and Ken Reed as co-producer. In addition, a number of associate producers joined the team, as did Dennis Collins, who brought his Georgetown Productions under the same roof and became the JBVP manager.

At an open house to celebrate the new firm, Johnny was proud to demonstrate his broadcast and special effects equipment and to show off his two new state of the art "music boxes"—a concert grand Yamaha piano and an Electone Yahama organ with synthesizers that could produce the sounds of an entire orchestra.

"I believe that there are hundreds of thousands of people who are hungry for good programming," says Johnny, "and I want to help fill the void they feel each time they turn on their television sets."

"John Biggers is a 'doer' in the truest sense of the word."

—*Dave Uribe*
Sacramento Bee

Besides travelogues and upbeat news features, Johnny believes there is a market for wholesome variety shows such as the ones filmed in the 1950s. His religious bent is evident in the gospel concerts and Biblically oriented videos he has produced, and his dedication to youth is the cornerstone of the programs he has taped for children, parents, teachers and businessmen about the drug problem facing today's boys and girls.

Another service he provides to young people includes tapes with a free enterprise theme.

"Video is a very educational way to show them just what an employer looks for when he hires someone," says John. "We can visually illlustrate what to expect in a job interview, how to dress and how to land that job they're after."

In addition, John has been working with many others in the electronic media field and has greatly expanded his area of expertise and his circle of friends. He is proud that Lee Roddy, author of such impressive works as *Grizzly Adams* and *The Lincoln Conspiracy*, is now involved with Johnny Biggers Video as a consultant and script writer. He is equally excited that he has purchased the international rights to Ethel Barrett's *Fanny Crosby*, the inspirational story of the blind hymn writer who wrote more than 6000 songs of devotion in her lifetime, including such favorites as "Blessed Assurance" and "Jesus is Calling." The live drama, presented by Nazarene actor D. Paul Thomas, is being filmed, and Johnny's video tape rights of that film will be available to Nazarene and Christians of all denominations throughout the world. Johnny also is inspired by the likes of billionaire Bunker Hunt, whose investment in Christianity resulted in the film "Jesus," another of Lee

Roddy's scripts and an evangelical tool that is shown worldwide.

A little closer to home, Johnny is pleased that he can now offer his new services and capabilities to the numerous charitable and civic groups he worked with in so many other capacities in the past. Along with Nola Joy Carello, popular Sacramento television and radio producer and talk show host, Johnny is producing public service announcements and documentaries and is making inroads into the advertising market. In addition, the company has video-taped microsurgeries at the University of California in Berkeley and has done training tapes for the Bank of America and other firms.

"It is estimated that, by 1990, more than 62 million American households will own video tape recorders," says Johnny. "JBVP already has a distribution network of video stores in the western United States and is in the position to have a major impact on the future of this new industry.

"More importantly, my video productions company has had a major impact on me. It's served as a bridge to yet another new beginning in my life and it's giving me the opportunity to make some good things happen that may not have occurred if I had never lived."

Al Howerstein, Chief of the State Office of Criminal Justice, presented Johnny with an award from the Sacramento Postmaster for outstanding video training tapes.

"No one could ask for a better business neighbor."

> —*Fred Carnie, Jr., Owner*
> *Fred E. Carnie and Son*

Johnny translates concern into action."

> —*Scott Mize, Col. Retired*
> *Jesuit High School*

"John Biggers puts his service and his money where his mouth is."

> *William Rutland*
> *Office of Commander*
> *United States Air Force*

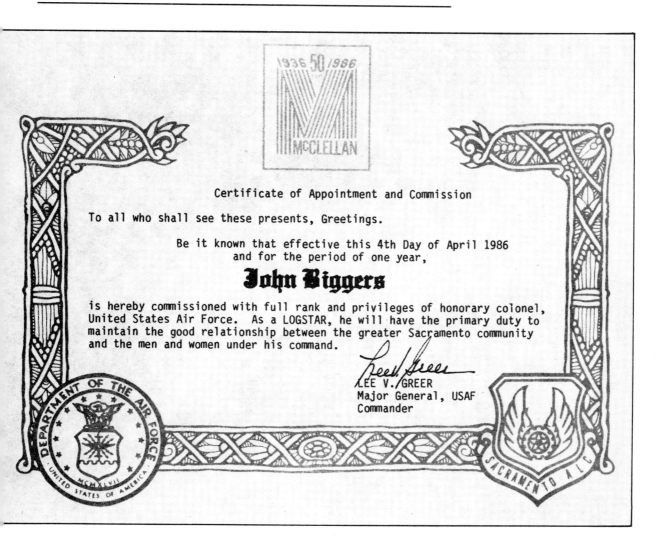

Certificate of Appointment and Commission

To all who shall see these presents, Greetings.

Be it known that effective this 4th Day of April 1986 and for the period of one year,

John Biggers

is hereby commissioned with full rank and privileges of honorary colonel, United States Air Force. As a LOGSTAR, he will have the primary duty to maintain the good relationship between the greater Sacramento community and the men and women under his command.

LEE V. GREER
Major General, USAF
Commander

JOHN A. BIGGERS
PRESIDENT

CHAPTER THIRTEEN

Tomorrow Begins Today

Johnny Biggers sees himself as a man standing on a bridge to tomorrow. It's a bridge that links a successful past with a promising future. It's a bridge that spans more than four decades of growth and accomplishment, and one that is paving the way for equally exciting and prosperous years to come. Yet it's a bridge John would never have considered crossing if it had not been for his children.

"It had been a long-time dream of mine to relocate and expand the business," he says, "but it's a step I would never have taken if my sons and daughters had not joined me.

"And now that they have, I know that, when 'my will matures,' the business will go on."

It had always been John's and Esther's hope that their children would be interested in joining the business. Merlene had become involved in the video productions enterprise, and Marlene, who had always wanted to work for her dad, had found her niche in the Gerlinger office after receiving a degree from the University of California at Berkeley. It was in the early 1980s that both of their sons had decided to make it a family affair.

Curt, upon graduating from high school, had entered Point Loma College on a wrestling scholarship. Originally an accounting major, he switched his course of study to business administration in his junior year, adding a minor in physical education. An eventful 1972 saw Curt join the Southwestern Life Insurance Company in May, graduate with honors in June and marry Jeanne Kettelhut in July. What followed was a highly successful management career of 10 years. Promotion followed promotion, exciting business travel abounded, and honors such as "Trainer of the Year" and as the youngest person in the company to ever receive the status of Charter Life Underwriter followed. To top those achievements, he studied for and received a chartered financial consultant's degree. And, by the time he was 30, he had earned the title of branch manager of Southwestern's Phoenix office.

Always one to place high expectations on himself, Curt knew that being successful was not a goal in itself.

"A person needs defined goals, a time frame and a road map," he says.

In 1982 Curt's road map directed him to 2020 K.

We are encouraged to learn from our failures. Add to that, 'Learn from your successes, and then duplicate success.'

Curt Biggers

Calvin had also enjoyed a stimulating career since he'd left high school. He'd joined Alpha Beta markets while working to earn a degree in law enforcement at California State University in Sacramento. Though it had been his intention to enter law school and pursue a career with the Federal Bureau of Investigation, Cal was quickly moving up the management ranks within the supermarket chain. He was promoted to manager of the produce and grocery departments and, by the time he was 28 years old, he had been named assistant manager of one of the stores in Sacramento. He was proud of his achievements. He was content in his choice of career. Yet, when his father approached him about making a move to Gerlinger's, Cal was excited about the prospect.

"I'd always felt that my father was a business genius," says Cal. "I've always admired the way he's able to motivate people. I knew I could learn from him. The opportunity to watch him in operation and to have him as my mentor was exciting."

John, who says that it is most rewarding as a parent to have his children *want* to work with him, nonetheless insisted that all of the department heads at Gerlingers interview Curt and Cal before they came on board. He was pleased that the entire management team agreed that the highly·successful and ambitious young men would be welcome additions to the staff.

"When Cal and I joined Gerlinger's, we were not running *from*,"

Marlene Biggers

says Curt. "We were running *to*."

"As kids it was always Curt and Cal against the world," says Cal, "and it's great that it's Curt and Cal together again."

Both men seem to thrive in their new positions and believe that there are many positive aspects to working in a family-owned business.

"We've always been a close-knit bunch," says Curt. "We work hard together and play hard together."

"Our father invested so much time, energy and money into our growth and development as children," says Cal, "and it's great that he now has the opportunity to see us operate as adults."

Both sons, who call their father "John" during working hours, enjoy the open and comfortable management style evident at Gerlinger's and are respected by customers and employees alike.

"There are few surprises because of the constant sharing," explains Cal.

Their skills were put to a test during the five and a half months that their father needed to recuperate from his open heart surgery.

"We went from rookies to hard-boiled veterans during that time," says Curt.

With the return of John Biggers, the management team decided it was time to accept the new challenges that had been but a dream before. They were ready to set a new goal, to relocate and to

Frank Mencarini, right, and Cal Biggers, below.

Shop Foreman Jim McBride, left, and Counter Sales Manager Don Henderson, below.

Engineering machinists Bob Scott, left, and Mike Morisette serve as project foremen for BIG. Below is Ron Mencarini, shop office coordinator.

expand.

After months of research and investigation, the Biggers chose a piece of property on the corner of Richards Boulevard and Sequoia Pacific as the new home of Biggers Industrial Gerlinger. A prime location, the new building is visible from Interstate Highway 5, which runs from Mexico to Canada, and just two miles from Interstate 80, which joins the Atlantic and the Pacific. In addition, the new site is just five miles from the Sacramento Airport, only one and one half miles from Yolo Port and is connected with the railway system by a spur the Biggers built on the property.

"We're right in the heart of the industrial section of Sacramento, but close enough to the retail area that we can still serve our regular customers," says Johnny. "And our proximity to the airport, the docks and the railway system has helped us establish a national and worldwide market for our industrial division."

The modern 50,000 sq. ft. building is four times larger than the old shop and was built with the expansion of the industrial division in mind. To reflect the growth of this division, the name of the firm has been changed to Biggers Industrial Gerlinger, often referred to as BIG.

"But we still have a service counter and an automotive section," Curt says. "It is Sacramento's longest sales counter."

"After all," he says with a grin, "you've got to stay with the

woman who brought you to the game."

In preparation for his company's increased industrial endeavors, John Biggers purchased a new heat treating oven from Gleason Engineering International to heat treat large to massive industrial engine crankshafts. In addition, a WRG Fusion build up processing machine that builds up and hardens crankshaft journals allows Biggers Industrial Gerlinger to refurbish giant locomotive-sized crankshafts up to 144 inches long.

In order to better prepare themselves for this technology, John and machinist Mike Morisette, a special projects engineer with BIG, traveled to several Pacific Rim countries for additional on-the-job training. Mike gained hands on experience during the trip with Bill and Jeff Gleason and his sister Sharon. The hard chrome plating technology, coupled with the Gleason process of crankshaft restoration, allows BIG to forge ahead of other processors on the nation's West Coast, in both technology and plant facilities.

Three machines are required for the highly-technical process. A fusion metal buildup machine provides the metal and wire buildup, and the Harcon Heat-treating Oven sets the process by a specially designed precision controlled heat treat and toughening procedure. An 11-ton, 28 ft. long Skou crankshaft and cylindrical grinder, custom-built to BIG's specifications by a manufacturer in Denmark, provides the precision grinding necessary to meet rigid control standards. The giant machine weighs 22,000 pounds. It takes up 28 lineal feet of floor space when at rest and 52 lineal feet when in operation.

In order to penetrate new markets and to accept the challenges they present, the BIG machinists and engineers must pursue constant training and course work and keep abreast of the changes and advancements in their fields. Shop foreman Jim McBride, a former college engineering instructor, requires five years experience of the technicians he hires. In addition, the staff receives cross-training with other industrial machine shops and, when college courses are required, BIG is willing to allow its employees time off—and in some cases financial aid—to further their education. Other instructional tools, such as manuals and, of course, videotapes, keep the BIG team on top in the competitive industry.

Walking through the immaculate new building that represented his dream and his future, Johnny Biggers surveyed his new domain and felt a rush of pride. Despite their immense sizes, the machinery almost seemed dwarfed by the roomy new quarters. He turned to the left and headed for the offices of Johnny Biggers Video Productions, also housed in these new lodgings. The fledgling company was outfitted with the highest quality broadcast equipment and held the promise of taking its place as a leader in the growing video industry. He opened the door to the studio, which he'd had the architect design with a stage and seating for almost 100 people. Performers were at their best when they had an audience, he knew.

He sighed, sat down in one of the auditorium-sized seats and stared at the stage before him. Suddenly that old Shakespearean phrase entered his mind. "All the world's a stage and all the men and women merely players."

Letting his imagination soar, he visualized scenes and people from his own life. His blessed parents and loving brothers and sis-

> *"Wisdom is knowing what to do next. Skill is knowing how to do it. Virtue is doing it."*

The entire family took part in groundbreaking ceremonies. In front, from left, are Ron and Merlene Mencarini, Marlene, Julie, next to her father Cal, Esther and Johnny. Seen in the background are Curt and his wife Jeanie and Barbara, Cal's wife.

555 SEQUOIA PACIFIC BLVD.

BIGGERS INDUSTRIAL GERLINGER

ters and the unforgettable childhood they had provided. His devoted wife Esther and the wonderful life they had shared. The sons and daughters who had made that life so worthwhile. George and Ella Gerlinger and the opportunity they'd extended an ambitious 17-year-old boy. His dedicated employees. His friends and fellow business men. They had all enriched his life so much. And of course, his God and his faith, which had sustained him through it all.

Johnny Biggers closed his eyes and was filled with a wonderful sense of accomplishment and contentment. Yet even as his heart swelled with feelings of pride and gratefulness, his mind was already considering tomorrow with its new excitement and promised challenges. What would the future bring? He wasn't certain, but that didn't dampen his anticipation.

He walked to the door, locked it behind him and headed for the parking lot to begin the journey home. And as he drove the short distance to River Park, he again found himself singing that well-loved chorus.

> Many things about tomorrow
> I don't seem to understand.
> But I know who holds tomorrow
> And I know who holds my hand.